How to Become an International Disaster Volunteer

D1713405

How to Become an International Disaster Volunteer

Michael Noone

Butterworth-Heinemann
An imprint of Elsevier

Butterworth-Heinemann is an imprint of Elsevier
The Boulevard, Langford Lane, Kidlington, Oxford OX5 1GB, United Kingdom
50 Hampshire Street, 5th Floor, Cambridge, MA 02139, United States

Notices
Knowledge and best practice in this field are constantly changing. As new research and
experience broaden our understanding, changes in research methods, professional practices, or
medical treatment may become necessary.

Practitioners and researchers must always rely on their own experience and knowledge in
evaluating and using any information, methods, compounds, or experiments described herein.
In using such information or methods they should be mindful of their own safety and the safety
of others, including parties for whom they have a professional responsibility.

To the fullest extent of the law, neither the Publisher nor the authors, contributors, or editors,
assume any liability for any injury and/or damage to persons or property as a matter of products
liability, negligence or otherwise, or from any use or operation of any methods, products,
instructions, or ideas contained in the material herein.

British Library Cataloguing-in-Publication Data
A catalogue record for this book is available from the British Library

Library of Congress Cataloging-in-Publication Data
A catalog record for this book is available from the Library of Congress

ISBN: 978-0-12-804463-6

For Information on all Butterworth-Heinemann publications
visit our website at https://www.elsevier.com/books-and-journals

Working together
to grow libraries in
developing countries

www.elsevier.com • www.bookaid.org

Publisher: Candice Janco
Acquisition Editor: Sara Scott
Editorial Project Manager: Hilary Carr
Production Project Manager: Punithavathy Govindaradjane

Typeset by MPS Limited, Chennai, India

Transferred to Digital Printing in 2017

DEDICATION

To Jackie and Mac — Thanks for allowing me to serve overseas and for the late nights working on this book. With all my love, Mike

CONTENTS

ABOUT THE AUTHOR

Michael Noone is a licensed paramedic and experienced disaster volunteer who responded to the 2010 earthquake in Haiti, the 2013 super typhoon in the Philippines, and the 2015 earthquakes in Nepal. He has been a firefighter, a public information officer, an ocean lifeguard and is currently a member of the United States federal DMAT (Disaster Medical Assistance Team) CA-1. With the CA-1 DMAT, he has provided medical care at the 2013 presidential inauguration and the 2014 presidential state of the union address. Mike has written articles that have been published in the *Journal for Prehospital and Disaster Medicine*. His full-time position is public health and disaster response and medical coordination for a five-county mutual aid region in Southern California.

ACKNOWLEDGMENTS

I deeply appreciate the opportunity to serve with Heartline Ministries in Haiti, with Hope Force International in the Philippines and Nepal, and with DMAT CA-1 in the United States.

Why This Book Was Written and How to Use It

I wrote this book because I wish that I had such a resource a decade ago when I started my efforts to work internationally as a disaster volunteer. I found many possible organizations but they all seemed to want previous experience, which I could not get until I was accepted into an organization. I could not crack this puzzle. Their websites stressed the benefits of volunteering but did not mention the downsides. I was not sure what character traits, training and equipment I should develop and acquire. I did not know what to expect on an actual deployment and I could not find anything which covered these topics and provided a plan to systematically achieve my goals. My hope is that this book will provide you with the candid information you need to become a prepared and effective international disaster volunteer.

You will find that there is a similar layout to all of the chapters in this book. In each, the majority of the writing describes specific aspects of international disaster volunteering. Interspersed are profiles of disaster response organizations and case studies of major incidents. As you read these profiles, ask yourself if you would be a good fit for that organization and vice versa. As you read the case studies, ask yourself what role you might have filled when responding to this disaster and what you would have needed to do so. Finally, at the end of several of the chapters, you will find recommended books as well as checklists to assist you in gathering supplies, information, and resources.

Lastly, the primary audience of this work is the reader interested in becoming a disaster volunteer. However, it is my hope that emergency managers and disaster planners who will be working with these volunteers will also pick this book up.

Please be aware that paid responders and government representatives can perceive disaster volunteers as liabilities: Untrained or underprepared, using scarce postdisaster food, water, housing and transportation while operating ineffectively, without telling anyone, not following local regulations, beginning or ending their missions on a whim, and failing to report their accomplishments or findings. Please do not fall into these bad habits and perpetuate this stereotype.

On the other side, government organizations from the United Nations down to your neighborhood council can be slow moving, overly concerned with paperwork and suspicious of responders they are not familiar with and do not directly control with a paycheck. Organizational hubris might prevent government representatives from admitting that we need outside assistance, or incline us to send the volunteers home while the community still needs help. Almost every disaster has had examples of squabbling between local and federal governments about whether resources were needed and who should provide them, while volunteer assets waited or were turned away.

To the prospective disaster volunteer I say: Please make sure you do not perpetuate negative volunteer stereotypes. The main goal of this book is to assist your efforts to be mentally, physically, logistically, and professionally prepared to be an asset rather than a liability in the disaster response. Join a reputable volunteer organization which has the infrastructure and resources to support you during the deployment. Make sure that your volunteer organization recognizes the importance of collaborating and coordinating with the existing or newly created emergency management structures which government agencies will be putting in place after a disaster strikes.

To my colleagues in emergency management—please admit that many of our poorer communities (even in the "developed" world) struggle on a day-to-day basis to provide food, shelter, and medical care for vulnerable populations. Do you think these inadequacies will magically improve after a catastrophe? Do not let professional conceit or loyalty to predisaster regulations cause you to turn away trained volunteer responders, even if it causes you work to manage their efforts.

I hope that this book will allow (well trained and prepared) volunteers and (thankful and cooperative) bureaucrats to appreciate the others' contributions and work together effectively.

Michael Noone

CHAPTER 1

Is Disaster Volunteering for You? The Rewards and Demands

Two roads diverged in a wood, and I—
I took the one less traveled by,
And that has made all the difference.

Robert Frost, The Road Not Taken

Thank you for your interest in helping others as an international disaster volunteer. I believe we have an innate and noble urge to support fellow humans (and animals, and the environment) in need. That desire manifests in a variety of ways. Most people will see news accounts of a disaster unfolding across the globe and their thoughts and prayers will go out to those affected. Many will take the time to make a personal financial donation. A smaller percentage will organize events to gather funds or supplies to send to the victims. And a very few individuals will grab their equipment and supplies, kiss their loved ones goodbye, and travel for hours or days to get to the disaster zone and begin directly helping those suffering. Who are these disaster responders and how do you become one?

Volunteers responding to Syrian refugees. Photo Courtesy of Mike Morse Photography.

FIVE W'S AND AN H

Even if you end up with a different focus I think it's helpful to recall, if possible, what initially drew your attention to international disaster volunteering.

> **TIP**
>
> As part of your development, I strongly urge you to begin keeping a journal, a folder, and/or an electronic record of the research, checklists, and articles you gather.

Who—Who did you see that made you interested in disaster relief work? Was it a news account? Or a movie, or a book? Can you remember the name of the organization to find out more about it? Or was it a friend, coworker, fellow student, or relative? Can you ask them about their experiences?

What—What do you want to do? Are you drawn to medical aspects of disaster volunteering? If so, what level will you start at and/or aspire to—technician, nurse, or physician? Are you interested in providing shelter, food, sanitation, animal care, communications, or clean water?

Where—Is there a particular area of the world in which you are interested in working? Africa, Asia, the Americas? Your common sense has already told you that poorer and less developed areas are usually more affected by catastrophes, so don't expect many disaster volunteering opportunities in Monte Carlo or Beverly Hills.

Why—What draws you to international disaster volunteering? Helping others in extreme situations? The teamwork required to set up a clinic or feeding station? Is it testing yourself under pressure? Are you considering it for a career?

When—This book will show that it takes time to prepare for and be accepted as a properly prepared disaster volunteer. So, if you have a "gap year" in your education approaching, retirement, or similar period of availability, begin organizing your efforts to volunteer now. If you have small children or are about to start a family, a new job, a new academic program, or new relationship—consider the major commitment required to do this type of extreme, short-notice volunteer work.

How long/How much—Considering the factors listed earlier (and many others we will discuss) how much time can you offer to these relief organizations for both training and deployments? Your time is worth money, but your money is also worth money. How much can you spare to pay for plane tickets, training, response supplies, etc.?

Think about these dynamics as we talk candidly about the pros and cons of disaster volunteering.

Port-au-Prince earthquake, 2010. Photo Courtesy of Author.

POTENTIAL BENEFITS

It takes courage to travel to another country and help strangers, especially when you aren't getting paid for this. In general it feels great to help others, but especially under these extreme circumstances.

Psychological Benefits

Let's address the adrenalin factor right away—it can be exciting to charge into a catastrophe, ready to help, challenging yourself in an extreme situation! Additionally, some of the benefits are the fulfillment of serving others, an increased self-confidence, lessons in teamwork, and the fellowship of generous people coming together in a crisis. These recollections and friendships will make you feel good for years to come. In addition to the emotional rewards, disaster volunteering has made me more grateful for the many positive things in my life, more flexible and resilient when faced with challenges, even at home, and more compassionate and empathetic in every situation.

Service Obligation

Depending on your religious or philosophical beliefs, you may feel you are fulfilling a duty to serve those in need. The group with which you chose to go could be an extension of these beliefs. In the mornings or evenings, if there is time, the team might have short reflections or discussions that deepen or illuminate your convictions, while sharing the day's experiences, positive and negative. You will leave the deployment with a greater appreciation for these principles and for the personalities of the unique individuals on your team.

Professional/Personal Development

Externally, your disaster volunteering may help your current career or lead to a new one. I believe my disaster volunteering experiences have impressed employers, demonstrating generosity, initiative, and self-sufficiency. A candidate who can calmly deal with obstacles in a disaster situation, working under pressure to achieve critical goals with their team, is usually a competitive applicant. (I've actually used that description in job interviews—it seems to be effective.) Finally, it is nice to have the admiration of my family and friends for my efforts, and my own disaster preparations for my community in earthquake-prone Southern California have been vastly improved by my real-world experiences. I have credibility when I urge others to be ready.

Hope Force International volunteers, Tacloban, Philippines, 2010. Photo Courtesy of Author.

The Professional Volunteer

I would like to address the "volunteer" versus "paid" versus "professional" divide I sometimes observe. A prejudice exists that someone must be paid to be a professional. This isn't true. Perceptive emergency managers have observed that being a paid responder does not ensure maturity, hard work, or competence. There are essential volunteers with thousands of hours of training and real-world disaster experiences. They prefer the flexibility of remaining unpaid responders even if they would quickly be snapped up as fulltime employees if they desired. Please, don't let the fact that you are not receiving wages for your efforts be an excuse to do less, train without intensity, or take your responsibilities lightly. In a disaster, the victim desperately seeking assistance doesn't care about the patch on your arm, the politics of your organization, or the amount of money you are (or aren't) getting paid to be there. That victim deserves competent, compassionate care whatever your status be.

DISADVANTAGES

On the negative side, from the mundane to the catastrophic, there are risks and costs associated with disaster volunteering.

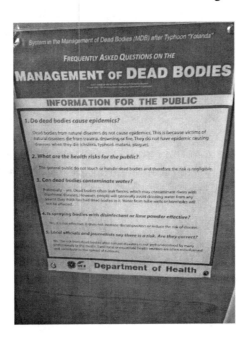

Public notice, Philippines 2010. Photo Courtesy of Author.

Are You There to Serve Yourself or Others?

First, a warning in recent years that an industry has sprung up catering to well-intentioned travelers with no specific skills who want to do volunteer work on their vacations. They pay a lot of money to fly to a poor country, work in an orphanage (or similar experience) for a week or two, take pictures with the cute children, and head home with the "personal development" box on their resume checked off. This has even been given a name: "voluntourism." Critics argue that some of these children's homes (or animal sanctuaries, etc.) exploit the residents to encourage the donations these tourists bring. These critics feel that regardless if the charity is sincere, that the cost of the trip would have been much better donated to a local sustainable development project, rather than creating an anecdote for someone's college entrance exam. The orphans are traumatized by a week of attention from this foreigner who then abandons them, or the construction work performed by the group is so shoddy that it must be rebuilt when they leave. International disaster volunteering has generally been free of these criticisms because after a disaster the need is undeniable, not created to encourage donations, and the majority of aid organizations send highly trained and experienced responders. However, it is always worth reminding yourself that your actions should benefit those you are serving more than they benefit you. Examining your motivations, would you still seek this experience if afterward you couldn't show/tell others anything about it? Since the photos in this book were taken during disasters, I have had to ask myself these questions as well.

Finances—Job—Family—School

Most of my trips have been self-financed and it is stressful to buy an expensive international plane ticket on very short notice. Similarly, I have always had to request last-minute vacation time from my employers. This requires a sympathetic and flexible supervisor and the knowledge that I may not have enough time later to take a personal, for-pleasure holiday. I came very close to losing a prized job over a disaster deployment and it permanently soured my relationship with that boss. Professors are usually open to letting their students delay assignments in order to serve as a disaster volunteer. However, I know from my personal experiences that despite my best intentions to get academic assignments done on the lengthy plane trips, I am usually too excited (going there) or too tired (coming home) to meet this goal. Similarly, despite the instructor's flexibility with deadlines and your desire to quickly jump back into academic life, you will probably return mentally and physically exhausted and it will be difficult for you to complete the missed work while simultaneously catching up on current projects. I learned this the hard way having had to withdraw from several classes after disaster volunteering trips.

Relationship Stress

These short-notice trips to disaster areas are hard not only on your budget, employer, and academic life (if enrolled) but also on your family and friends, who will worry about you the entire time you are away. Some people will never understand your drive to travel to and work in a disaster stricken area. This anxiety is only amplified by the limited phone/Internet connections in most affected regions. I was in Nepal when a major aftershock struck after the catastrophic 2015 earthquake. We were unharmed and able to communicate and the volunteer organization I was with did a great job of quickly updating the team's families. However, for weeks after I returned the trip other friends, colleagues, and acquaintances stopped me to say how worried they had been when they saw the news reports and thought I might have been hurt or killed. I hadn't thought to give my social media account passwords to someone else back home so that once word got back to my family, they could announce that I was safe to others outside that inner circle.

TIP

Establish a communication plan before you deploy, not just for your close friends and family, but also for your coworkers and acquaintances.

Please don't underestimate the emotional toll your disaster volunteer efforts will take on the people who care about you. Like military service or other commitments that remove someone from their homes, disaster deployments put romantic relationships under particular stress. Your significant other may not support this endeavor 100%, leading to resentment and conflict. It is not uncommon, especially during longer trips, for existing romances to fail nor is it unheard of for fleeting ones to spring up among the disaster volunteers. All of this is to say that clear communication with your significant other about feelings and expectations before, during (if possible) and after the deployment will be critical to maintaining the relationship.

Hazards

While on deployment, there are a variety of physical and psychological hazards. These include limited or contaminated food and water, lack of sleep/shelter, exposure to hazardous environments such as collapsed buildings or damaged roads, the possibilities of looters or civil unrest, and the inability to access timely medical care or evacuation if you are injured. Psychologically, you will be operating on limited sleep and nutrition, often under chaotic, hot, wet, and dirty conditions, with your small team of diverse individuals who you may not know well, while dealing with a local population who are grieving for lost relatives, friends, homes, and livelihoods.

Both the aid givers and aid receivers are under tremendous emotional stress and there are times on every deployment when I have asked myself why I was volunteering or why everyone else on my team was so irritating (and I am sure they felt the same way about me).

Missing person, Philippines 2013. Photo Courtesy of Author.

Posttraumatic Stress

Lastly, I have always felt a psychological let-down when I returned from a disaster deployment. I'm sure this is an element of posttraumatic stress, despite, relatively speaking, all my disaster deployments having gone smoothly. Still, one day I'm helping staff a clinic in a badly damaged hospital, scrambling to find electricity and medication for patients who have been sleeping in the streets. I'm incredibly grateful for a 5-minute break to eat a granola bar or a pan of clean water to wash my face. I'm assisting victims with their life-changing tragedies. Then my deployment period ends. Jarringly, after an (exhausting) international plane trip, I'm dropped back into the routines of "normal" life—the phone company is calling because my bill is late. My boss wants to know if I'll be at the staff meeting this afternoon. I can't sleep due to jetlag and I'm baffled that my friends are so intrigued by celebrity gossip or sports scores when children are homeless halfway across the globe.

TIP

If you want to keep your friends, please control any well-meaning but condescending impulses to lecture them on the shallowness of their interests now that you're back from saving the world. Channel your good intentions into raising awareness and donations for the disaster victims instead.

Coming home, the contrast can be shocking, often more so because the scenes of injuries and deaths you witnessed will stay with you for months and years. You may need to seek professional counseling to process some of these experiences, which is another time and financial cost.

Courtesy of Mike Morse Photography.

Age

While there is no optimal age for disaster volunteers, I have found the majority of them have been in their twenties to fifties. Don't worry if you are outside that category. Volunteers who are younger than 18–21 years old may have difficulty finding an organization to sponsor them for legal and liability reasons. Be patient! You will see that most disaster response organizations are highly selective for who they choose to accept. Methodically work your way through the recommendations in this book to increase your personal readiness, volunteer experience, and training and you will find a year or two has quickly passed and more groups will be interested in you. For older volunteers—many of you are blessed with additional time, financial resources, life experience, and maturity than your younger peers. You may be able to get required training completed more quickly than someone trying to balance school and/or childcare commitments. And, taking several weeks off with no notice to deploy internationally may not be as difficult at this stage in your life. However the physical and mental stresses of working in a disaster zone cannot be overstated. You will probably doing hard labor in hot and humid condition for 12–16 hours a day, with limited food and water and poor sleeping conditions at night. If your overall health and fitness are just average (or worse) for your age, take a year or two to improve your strength, flexibility, and stamina so you won't be the weak link on your team.

CONCLUSION

You have considered the pros and cons of international disaster volunteering. Hopefully you have begun to fill a folder or notebook with your disaster lists and questions. Next is the research you will want to do on the various organizations doing disaster response. Let's get to it!

Organizational Profile

International Red Cross Committee

Used with permission: ICRC.

The International Committee of the Red Cross (ICRC) is one of the oldest and most prominent international NGO (nongovernmental organization) disaster relief organizations. Its goal is to assist those caught up in armed conflicts around the world. However the ICRC, or representatives from its 189 national societies like the Canadian Red Cross, regularly responds to natural disasters as well.

TIP

Start an acronym list in your folder so you will recall what NGO and ICRC mean when you see them again.

The ICRC is guided by seven principles—humanity, impartiality, neutrality, independence, voluntary service, unity, and universality. It was founded after the 1859 battle of Solferino, where French and Piedmontese forces were attempting to drive the Austrian army out of Italy. A visiting 31-year-old Swiss businessman, Jean Henri Dunant, saw that thousands of wounded soldiers had been left without aid. He arranged care for the wounded from nearby towns, especially from local woman and children. Using the slogan "Tutti fratelli" (all are brothers), Dunant convinced the aid givers to treat soldiers from either side without discrimination and bought supplies with his own money. He was also able to get captured Austrian doctors released by the French to assist in the response.

Dunant wrote about his involvement in the memoir *Un Souvenir de Solferino (A Memory of Solferino)* and promoted a plan to form relief agencies around the world. He gathered support for his proposals and in 1863 the Geneva Society for Public Welfare founded the International Committee for the Relief of the Wounded (ICRW) which eventually became the ICRC. In 1864 concurrent diplomatic efforts led to the creation of the "Convention for the Amelioration of the Condition of the Wounded and Sick in Armed Forces in the Field" also known as the Geneva Convention and the ICRC was given responsibility for investigating and reporting violations. In 1901 for his efforts, Dunant won the first Nobel Peace Prize.

It is worth noting that due to personal business failures and tension with one of the other cofounders, Dunant was forced out of the ICRC in 1868 and he spent the rest of his life trying to rehabilitate his image and rejoin the Red Cross. Simply because an organization is devoted to the noble cause of helping others doesn't mean that jealousy, rivalry, poor financial judgment, and other less than admirable human impulses won't raise their ugly heads. Remember this.

As noted earlier, the ICRC maintains a strong emphasis on problems stemming from wars and other violent conflicts. However, many of the national chapters such as the American Red Cross and the Mexican Cruz Roja work primarily on responding to emergencies and disasters of all types, from small to large, within their nations and internationally. These response activities may include assisting victims displaced by house fires, flooding, or storms, by providing food, shelter, and other needs. Most national Red Cross organizations have comprehensive training programs broken down into short modules. You can focus on an area, such as shelter management or medical assistance, which interests you and build up expertise. These skills will be valuable in domestic and international disaster responses. Additionally, because of its global operations, Red Cross personnel almost always have existing local contacts and organizational support when they enter a disaster zone.

Like any institution of its size, the Red Cross has faced criticism. The ICRC has been faulted for keeping Geneva Convention violations confidential while they attempt to negotiate resolutions with the offending governments. The ICRC feels that without this confidentiality they would lose access to prisoners and war zones but others argue their discretion enables the abusers. Likewise, national chapters have been condemned in the media for fundraising techniques, recordkeeping, or spending habits. The Red Cross is a large bureaucracy managing massive resources, and it has been accused of initiating responses too slowly or failing to modify practices in the face of changed circumstances.

Symbols of ICRC chapters: the Red Cross, the Red Crescent, and the Red Crystal (used in place of the Star of David). Used with permission: ICRC.

Before spending a year or two of your life volunteering with the Red Cross, or any other organization, do your research. Read the promotional material distributed by your affiliate, but find independent reviews and news accounts of the national and local chapter activities and priorities. Attend an orientation meeting and chat with more seasoned volunteers. Would you see yourself training and responding with them? Do the Red Cross philosophies and activities match your interests? If there are disagreements regarding Red Cross decisions and actions, can you live with them?

Despite the occasional controversies, the Red Cross remains one of the preeminent international disaster response and relief agencies. Because of its methodical training program and global reach, thousands of international disaster volunteers and paid workers have gotten their start with the ICRC and its affiliate societies.

Disaster Case Study:

Hurricane Katrina

Hurricane Katrina was a massive Caribbean cyclone, which made landfall as a Category 4 storm on August 29, 2005 over the city of New Orleans (population 1.3 million), and coastal areas of the states of Louisiana, Mississippi, and Alabama in particular. It is considered the third strongest hurricane to hit the United States and the most financially damaging, causing 108 billion USD in damages and approximately 1800 fatalities. Initial sustained maximum winds of 175 mph (280 kmh) and a storm surge of 12–14 ft overwhelmed a system of embankments and floodwalls designed to protect the low-lying city from flooding. Subsequent investigations showed that to save money these flood control levees were designed and built with substandard materials which contributed to their failure.

Saffir-Simpson Hurricane Scale			
Category	Winds (MPH)	Damage	Storm Surge
1	74 - 95	**Minimal:** Damage to unanchored mobile homes, vegetation & signs. Coastal road flooding. Some shallow flooding of susceptible homes.	4 - 5 feet
2	96 - 110	**Moderate:** Significant damage to mobile homes & trees. Significant flooding of roads near the coast & bay.	6 - 8 feet
3	111 - 130	**Extensive:** Structural damage to small buildings. Large trees down. Mobile homes largely destroyed. Widespread flooding near the coast & bay.	9 - 12 feet
4	131 - 155	**Extreme:** Most trees blown down. Structural damage to many buildings. Roof failure on small structures. Flooding extends far inland. Major damage to structures near shore.	13 - 18 feet
5	More than 155	**Catastrophic:** All trees blown down. Some complete building failures. Widespread roof failures. Flood damage to lower floors less than 15 feet above sea level.	Greater than 18 feet

Previous well-publicized risk—hazard analyses had identified the probability of a catastrophic hurricane-related flooding event in New Orleans. Although as with most major storms, the impacted area had 24–48 hours of warning, some residents were depending on a change of path by the hurricane to spare them from its effects. This psychological phenomenon of "It won't happen to me." is not uncommon and is a major cause of a failure to prepare for disasters adequately. People from all walks of life, including elected officials, business owners, and even emergency managers, can fall victim to this wishful thinking.

As with most disasters, multiple hazards and human shortcomings were evident during Katrina. Most of the deaths were among vulnerable populations (the already sick, the elderly, the disabled, the poor, and the children) caused by drownings or exacerbations of their preexisting medical conditions. Emergency managers failed to adequately plan for these residents and in some cases their guardians abandoned them. Power failed, and along with it air-conditioning, communications, and critical healthcare equipment. The media played up reports of looting, assaults, and violence. Subsequent investigations revealed those occurrences were relatively rare and the classification of "looting" is arguably inaccurate if someone who is unable to get food/water from disaster responders takes those lifesaving supplies from a flooded store. Municipal water supplies were unable to maintain pressure and contaminated by spilled fuel, sewage, and other chemicals. Most major roads were damaged and inoperable. There were political tensions and accusations of favoritism and indifference between politicians at the local, state, and national level.

Hundreds of aid organizations responded to Katrina, from large to small, government, military, corporate, faith based, student-led, and informal. With varying degrees of effectiveness/coordination with local, state, and federal authorities, these groups provided medical care, shelter, food, water, debris management and cleanup, animal rescue and treatment, psychological and spiritual support, and economic assistance.

The Katrina disaster had many examples of heroism from individual responders such as Ken Bellau (a civilian who rescued over 400 people in a borrowed boat) and US Coast Guard helicopter personnel who plucked hundreds of residents off roofs after they were stranded by rising floodwaters. However the overwhelming lesson was the failure of governmental authorities to prepare, respond, and coordinate the relief efforts.

Recommended Reading

Five Days at Memorial: Life and Death in a Storm-Ravaged Hospital
Sheri Finks

This is an acclaimed and thoroughly researched book describing the efforts of staff and patients at New Orleans' Memorial Hospital to survive the rising waters and deteriorating conditions during Hurricane Katrina. It offers vivid and disturbing accounts of the life and death decisions made under hellish conditions by the medical providers, the patients and their families.

Following the storm, as electrical power, potable water, plumbing, and air-conditioning failed in this large inner-city hospital, staff desperately called authorities and their corporate management for information and resources. They were not given support. Patients on ventilators had to be resuscitated by hand. Hospital personnel, patients, and family members suffered horribly from the heat, humidity, lack of food and clean water, and raw sewage backing up in the rooms. Some caregivers abandoned their duties to return to their own homes and families, also seriously affected by the storm. There were reports of roving bands of looters, killers, and rapists on the streets outside and the city was unable to provide any police or security for the building.

Eventually, after days of worsening conditions, a rapid, disorganized evacuation begun. Fearing that some patients were too sick to move, doctors gave several of them large doses of painkillers—an action for which they later faced legal consequences and ethical questions.

The author also contrasts the decisions and actions of the Memorial staff with those of other medical facilities in New Orleans who arguably handled the extreme conditions better.

When you read it, ask yourself what you might have done in their situation and what lessons can be found for future responses.

CHAPTER 2

Finding and Choosing the Right Volunteer Organization

Never doubt that a small group of thoughtful, committed citizens can change the world; indeed, it's the only thing that ever has.

Margaret Mead

You have evaluated the pros and cons and you have decided that disaster volunteering is a good fit for you now or in the near future. It's time to look for the organization with which you want to volunteer. I also highly recommend that you prepare for disasters in your own community, on your own or as part of a local group.

START YOUR RESEARCH

Your selection of a group to join is just as important as a major educational or career choice so I recommend you use your folder(s), either electronic or paper, to save profiles, articles, notes, etc. When you are overseas, in a disaster zone, your life and safety are in their hands. Don't take this search lightly.

Just as we will discuss with disaster supplies, there are organizations which fall into the "good, better, and best" categories. And, especially as you begin your disaster volunteering endeavors, the "good" option may be most appropriate for you. For example, you may find that a local faith based or university group travels to an underdeveloped area to do regularly scheduled short-term medical, dental, or eye clinics. Or you volunteer to do logistics or security in a music festival at a remote location.

How to Become an International Disaster Volunteer.

While this is not officially "disaster volunteering," this is a great introduction to the skills and supplies you will need for an actual disaster. And, it will demonstrate to the organizations with which you will be applying that you have real-world experience working with a team in austere conditions (no power/no water/no supporting infrastructure).

Courtesy of Mike Morse Photography.

You may have an organization already in mind—perhaps you saw them on the news working in a disaster. This time of research should reveal if you are a good fit for them and vice versa. Take *Medicin Sans Frontiers/Doctors Without Borders*. Undoubtedly, they are one of the best known and most respected disaster response medical organizations in the world. They are also looking for highly qualified medical professionals like senior emergency room/trauma personnel who have previous experience working in austere environments. If you do not fit that description, it is highly unlikely that you would be accepted by such an organization and if you were you would probably be overwhelmed by what they expected of you. You wouldn't try to go from shooting basketball in your driveway to playing on a world championship team—give yourself and the organization the preparation you both deserve.

Scheduled Volunteer Experiences
Many years ago, I found a local church group which organized an annual 10-day medical mission to the mountains of the Dominican

Republic and applied to participate. We would be without electricity and would be using untreated and unheated water from streams during the time while we operated a temporary clinic in a small village. One great advantage was that the trip was scheduled months in advance and I had time to save money for an airline ticket, purchase equipment and notify my employer and friends. While I had visited poorer areas in the world as a tourist and felt prepared for what I would see and how we would live, traveling with a team and with an assignment was a completely different experience.

Before being accepted to such a team you will probably be interviewed and evaluated to see if you are suitable in your skills, and mental and physical readiness. The team leader will describe their goals and behavioral principles. You will be expected to follow the team's rules and schedule, not your own wishes. On a personal trip, if I want to sleep in, or go for an early morning jog, I do so, but as part of a team I followed the guidelines needed to get the day's tasks accomplished. These rules may include a request to abstain from alcohol and/or profanity or give you clothing directions to avoid offending the local population. If you are volunteering at a festival or athletic event, you will be reminded that during your shifts you are there to work, not to participate in the activities. You may have to wear a vest or an unflattering uniform to ensure that festival participants know you are part of the event. Don't be the volunteer who disobeys these rules or demands exceptions.

During the Dominican Republic mission, I had a great time but the experience forced me to confront many of my personal pet peeves. I love to take a hot shower every day but couldn't do so for nearly two weeks. I dislike talking about my feelings in public but the group gathered each night for an often emotional debrief and discussion. I hate sleeping in the same room with a group of snoring strangers (or friends) but I survived that as well. Likewise, the group provided me with a list of recommended personal supplies. This was a great introduction to disaster survival packing and I used my experiences and what I saw my fellow volunteers bringing to add and subtract from that list for upcoming deployments. This first medical deployment confirmed that I wanted to be a disaster volunteer, but also gave me a taste of working with the team dynamic in extraordinary conditions and helped me identify the areas that would particularly cause me stress in future trips (hygiene, snoring, and emotional sharing).

Courtesy of Mike Morse Photography.

TIP

A multiyear, tiered approach may be best for you. Year One find a local group planning a volunteer trip or outdoor special event in your home country, Year Two join a scheduled international volunteer mission, and Year Three find an international disaster organization with which to deploy.

Types of Volunteer Organizations

While we often visualize a mobile trauma unit treating patients after a disaster, there are many areas other than medical care that need assistance when calamity strikes. These include reestablishing temporary or permanent shelter; distributing food and bottled water; testing, treating, and repairing the damaged municipal water systems; providing communications capabilities such as amateur radio to the area; assisting animals affected by the disaster; and economic assistance such as microloans or hiring locals for short-term employment clearing debris.

Most people begin their search for volunteer organizations on the Internet. As noted earlier, you may have heard of several groups. There are more listed at the end of a number of chapters in this book. Visit their websites. Download or print out their mission statements, geographical and vocational areas of focus (type of relief work—i.e., medical vs water sanitation), volunteer requirements and any other specifications which set them apart. Once you have looked at the groups whose names you already knew, use a search engine to find others.

Decide what area you would like to help with and where it is realistic you could assist. Do you want something tied to your current/future career or would you like to keep your paid work and your volunteer efforts completely separate? Below is an emergency function chart used by the US government. It covers activities they believe are critical to address after a disaster and if you search hard enough you will probably find multiple disaster volunteer groups which focuses on each of these needs.

United States/FEMA List of Emergency Response Functions (ESFs)

- ESF 1: Transportation
- ESF 2: Communications
- ESF 3: Public Works and Engineering
- ESF 4: Firefighting
- ESF 5: Emergency Management
- ESF 6: Mass Care, Housing and Human Services
- ESF 7: Resource Support
- ESF 8: Public Health and Medical Services
- ESF 9: Urban Search and Rescue
- ESF 10: Oil and Hazardous Materials Response
- ESF 11: Agriculture and Natural Resources
- ESF 12: Energy
- ESF 13: Public Safety and Security
- ESF 14: Long Term Community Recovery and Mitigation
- ESF 15: External Affairs

In addition, here is the way the United Nations addresses disaster needs in their Cluster system:

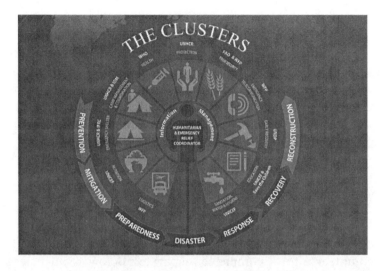

Are you familiar with how your nation organizes its disaster response activities? Will it be led domestically by a national emergency management agency like the United States' FEMA (Federal Emergency Management Agency) and internationally by an outreach agency like US OFDA (Office of Foreign Disaster Assistance) a division of USAID (the United States Agency for International Development). Perhaps in your country these efforts are the responsibility of a civil defense agency or the military. There are lots of acronyms and abbreviations (ESF, WHO, UNICEF, etc.), start looking them up and keeping that definition list. When you are in the company of disaster responders they will use them extensively and you may feel like they are speaking a foreign language.

While you are researching these disaster response groups take note of how large they are, how many years they have been in existence, and their philosophical or religious beliefs. Do you agree with their motives and methods? Use a search engine to find news articles about real-world responses. A group may have faced controversies over their activities or leadership. Don't rule them out because of a few bad things you see—look at the big picture. There are websites like guidestar.org or give.org, which may provide additional information such as how much of each organization's funds go into disaster relief, how much to overhead costs, etc. Don't rely on just one source, but seek out several to get a full picture of how the group works.

> **TIP**
>
> Although you can certainly change your mind later, decide whether you want your volunteer activities to be in the same field as your current or planned career, or if you want to keep those areas separated and do something completely different.

Find out how long the response group has existed, how often they deploy, whether their volunteers pay for their own travel costs, the size of their volunteer/paid staff, the size of their deployment teams, required training, equipment, and experience.

Input From Family/Friends/Employer

Ask your loved ones with which types of disaster response they are comfortable with you volunteering. For example, they may be fine with you assisting a poor but stable country after an earthquake or hurricane. However, they may be worried about you bringing back a disease if you respond to an epidemic or you being kidnaped if you are helping in an area of war or civil unrest.

Here are other examples of volunteer activities after a disaster: fuel distribution for generators, vehicles, and stoves; engineering and architectural evaluation of damaged buildings; private pilots bringing in supplies; managing and distributing donations; human resources and volunteer management; legal services and advice; and psychological counseling and spiritual support.

PERSONAL READINESS

It doesn't make sense to spend time, effort, and money to become an international disaster volunteer while leaving yourself and your loved ones vulnerable to disasters in your own community. You should have an emergency plan and supplies in place for your own home, work, and car before jetting off to help others. Without spending much, you can vastly improve your readiness. And once you educate yourself, you can spread the message of disaster preparedness in your community and diminish the effects of any widespread catastrophe.

Port-au-Prince 2010. Photo Courtesy of Author.

Risk—Hazard Analysis

The first step in the process is a risk and hazard analysis, which is exactly what it sounds like. Most disasters have common elements: shortages of power, food, and water, e.g., but your location may be particularly susceptible to winter storms, flooding, earthquakes, tornadoes, or other situations with unique features. Some questions to ask: First, in the past, what disasters and risks have occurred in your community? Wildfires, hurricanes, industrial chemical releases, snowstorms? Second, how much prior notice do you anticipate having? (For storms, we usually know 2—3 days in advance, while for earthquakes no notice.) You shouldn't take that early warning for granted, but your emergency plan might factor in a more leisurely packing and departure schedule as a hurricane approaches versus a sudden power outage. Third, are there distinctive challenges to these hazards (extreme heat or cold, the need to seal windows/doors from a chemical plant leak, etc.) which may require special equipment or knowledge? For example, do you have alternate methods to heat or cool your house without electricity from the municipal grid. Fourth, are there special characteristics to you and your family: animal (pet food, medications, kennels, horse trailers), human (special diets, medications, glasses and contact lenses, small valuables and important documents) that you should take into account? Your city, county, state, or national government offices of emergency management or civil defense should be able to provide a list of common hazards and vulnerabilities for your region to help you plan. Similarly, while disaster planning and supply checklists are provided here, those government offices may be able to provide more detailed resources.

Supplies and Equipment

The concept behind the semi-humorous Murphy's Law ("What can go wrong will go wrong, probably at the worst possible time.") dictates that if you truly need something to function, and you only have one, it will fail. Likewise, there is a motto from the military regarding critical equipment: "Two is one and one is none." By this they mean that if something is really important you should have two of them at a minimum.

Once you have an idea of the risks and special factors you are facing, come up with a plan and a list of supplies. The planning and supply checklists are provided here but a few recommendations and philosophies first. Don't get overwhelmed by the length and cost of the lists. Like many things in life it is better to start small and scale up, and for almost every situation there are good, better, and best solutions.

Are you worried about charging your mobile phone or powering other devices in your home after an electrical system failure? A good and inexpensive solution could be a personal solar panel or small hand crank radio with charging ports. A more powerful, but costly purchase would be a portable internal combustion generator, able to run several larger appliances at once. For this you will need to have electrical cords, sufficient fuel and oil, and good ventilation. The most seamless response for electrical failure is to have your home wired to a permanent backup generator, solar power, or large capacity battery, which automatically activates when needed. That "best" solution is very expensive and requires professional installation and maintenance. If the "best" and "better" categories are out of your budget or desire, there are plenty of good and affordable solutions and thorough emergency plans usually include redundant methods to achieve each goal anyway (i.e., an inexpensive solar charger in addition to the portable generator, in case it fails).

Maslow's Hierarchy of Needs

Take a look at the following two versions of Maslow's Hierarchy of Needs as you consider your personal preparedness for a disaster. The wide base show the elements you must have to survive (air, food, and water) and as you move upwards to the point, they show items or concepts you can add once those elemental physical needs have been covered.

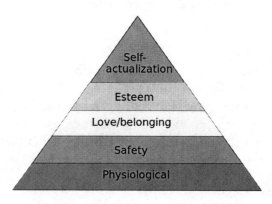

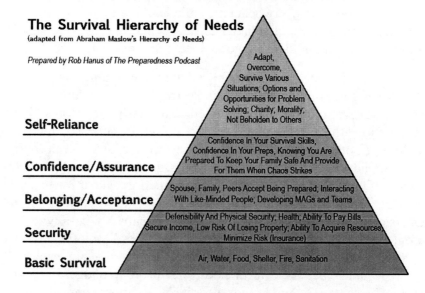

Categorize your emergency planning and supply lists using the places in which you spend the most time along with the hazards you face. Most of us have a home, dorm, or apartment, plus we spend significant time on public transit or in a car commuting to and from work or school. Those are three distinct locations and it would be optimal to have survival kits (of varying size and composition) available at every stage of the day. For example, living in Southern California and concerned with earthquakes, I assume, if I weren't badly injured, that if the roads were damaged by a quake I would need to walk (perhaps 10–15 miles) home or to safety. Therefore in my house, car, and office I always have walking shoes, enough food and water for a long hike, and a cheap backpack to carry these supplies (as well as an inexpensive crank radio, etc.). The good news is that many of the personal preparedness supplies and techniques are transferable to your international disaster volunteering. Buying bottles of water purification tablets for your home and car kits? Buy an extra bottle and throw it in your deployment bag. Or, create a detailed checklist for your deployment bag that says: "Take water purification tablets from car kit." Just make sure everything goes back to their original locations when you are done.

Resilience and Community

New research has shown what common sense always told us: an important element of disaster survival and recovery (also known as resilience) is the strength of the community. Do you know your neighbor and their phone numbers? After a disaster, you may have extra batteries and he/she may have extra canned goods or only one of you may have a solar cell phone charger—do you know them well enough to share resources and psychological support for your mutual benefit? The time to form these (even casual) contacts is before a disaster.

The goals of these efforts are to have you ready for a disaster in your own community before traveling to help someone else AND to let you leave with the peace of mind that if a disaster happens in your neighborhood while you are gone your loved ones would have the right supplies and knowledge to get by without you.

Organizational Profile

International Amateur Radio Union

Analyses after every major disaster identify that established methods of communications fail and alternatives, such as amateur radio, are vitally important. Like the International Committee for the Red Cross, the International Amateur Radio Union is an umbrella organization for over 150 national chapters of amateur (HAM) radio organizations around the world, with several sections devoted to public service and emergency response.

In the early 20th century, as radio became the new and dominant form of communication, commercial providers assumed that more power and larger antennas were the only ways to send messages over long distances. However, through experimentation, amateurs discovered that short-wave signals on modest equipment could be heard across the world. There were efforts to take these short-wave frequencies away from amateurs and commercialize these bands. The International Amateur Radio Union and its many national leagues (such as the Amateur Radio Relay League—ARRL, in the United States) were founded to preserve amateur radio. As the hobby developed, the chapters established strict rules for licensure and operation (e.g., you cannot charge for or profit from transmissions) and their utility became evident during emergencies when other forms of communication such as cellular and hardwire telephone and Internet failed or became overwhelmed.

There are several explanations for the association of the word "ham" with amateur radio but most believe it was originally a pejorative term referring to ham-fisted former telegraph operators who had transitioned to operating amateur radio poorly. With a few years the negative connotation had disappeared and practitioners proudly called themselves "HAMs."

During a disaster, HAM operators at hospitals, shelters, supply distribution depots, and command posts can relay critical information. Additionally, many emergency response HAM groups volunteer at marathons and other athletic and special events, disaster drills, etc. This allows them to keep up their skills, maintain contacts with emergency managers, and in the event of an emergency at the event, their HAM capabilities serve as a redundant form of communication.

There are specific subgroups of the ARRL which are focused on emergency response, such as RACES (Radio Amateur Civil Emergency Service) and ARES (Amateur Radio Emergency Services). Usually these organizations pair up with emergency responders such as aid groups, hospitals, and disaster management agencies. A downside is that many HAMs have to purchase their own equipment but if technology and communications are your volunteering interests, Amateur Radio may be a great fit for you.

Disaster Case Study:

The Vargas Landslides, Venezuela 1999

Vargas is a coastal state in the north of Venezuela. In almost all areas steep mountain ranges extend to the ocean's edge. Because of this, terrain which is flat and inhabitable, such as shoreline riverbed fans, is densely populated even if the residents are at risk from flooding and the buildings may be constructed on alluvial sediment rather than bedrock. Throughout the month of December 1999, the region experienced heavy rains, saturating soil in the mountains. This culminated in extremely heavy storms from December 14th to 16th and at approximately 8 p.m. local time the first debris flow of up to 10 ft (3.3 m) swept toward the downstream communities at up to 30 mph (48 kmh). These debris flows had large boulders (up to 11.3 m × 5.0 m × 3.5 m) which were especially devastating to bridges and buildings. In one community alone (the Caraballeda fan), debris accumulated up to 20 ft in height and with a mass of 1.8 million cubic meters, crushing and drowning residents and blocking access to help them. More than 10,000 people died in the disaster. 300 miles of roads were wiped out. Approximately 8000 houses were destroyed and a quarter million people affected.

Think critically about this incident and do a Risk–Hazard Analysis. If a wall of mud and debris swept through your neighborhood at 8 p.m. at night, what effects would it have? Where would children and adults be—at school and work, or in their beds asleep or in their homes, but awake? How would the mud and debris be dangerous to work in and around—with hazardous chemicals mixed in from houses and businesses, along with sewage, glass, and sharp construction wreckage? What type of personal equipment or clothing should you bring to South America for a hot, rainy, dirty, dangerous environment? Would you expect municipal water systems to keep functioning and/or be accessible? How do you think your volunteer group would get you and your supplies to the site if the roads were unusable? There were multiple major debris flows over several days—how would you keep your team safe and aware of these hazards? How would you communicate with your team in the region and your contacts many miles away if the cellular and landline phone systems were not working? What types of relief organizations responded to this tragedy? What challenges did they face?

Checklist:

Personal Preparedness
- 4–5 Day supply of nonperishable food (dried fruit, canned tuna fish, peanut butter, etc.)
- Can opener
- Paper plates, plastic cups and utensils, paper towels
- Moist towelettes, garbage bags and plastic ties for personal sanitation
- Water—at least a gallon per person, per day for drinking and hygiene
- First aid kit
- Prescription medication and glasses
- Sleeping bag or warm blanket for everyone in your family
- Change of clothes to last for at least 3 days, including sturdy shoes; consider the weather where you live
- Matches in a waterproof container
- Toothbrush, toothpaste, soap, and other personal items
- Feminine hygiene supplies
- Fire extinguisher
- Wrench or pliers to turn off utilities
- Dust mask, and plastic sheeting and duct tape, to help filter contaminated air
- Battery-powered or hand-cranked radio and extra batteries
- Flashlights and extra batteries
- Cell phone with charger, extra battery, and solar charger
- Whistle to signal for help
- Household chlorine bleach and medicine dropper (when diluted nine parts water to one part bleach, bleach can be used as a disinfectant. Or in an emergency, you can use it to treat water by using 16 drops of regular household liquid bleach per gallon of water. Do not use scented, color safe or bleaches with added cleaners.)
- Local maps
- Cash or traveler's checks
- Emergency reference material such as first aid book or information from www.ready.gov
- Important family documents such as copies of insurance policies, ID, and bank records in a waterproof, portable container
- Pet supplies
- Formula and diapers
- Paper and pencil
- Books, games, or puzzles (let your kids pick these out themselves!)
- Your child's favorite stuffed animal or security blanket
- Pet food and extra water for your pet

Source: United States Federal Emergency Management Agency.

CHAPTER 3

Developing Relevant Training and Education for Deployments

The measure of intelligence is the ability to change.

— *Albert Einstein*.

BRIEF HISTORY OF DISASTER RESPONSE

Throughout human history there have always been disasters such as floods, famine, wars, earthquakes, plagues, and devastating fires. Many historians believe that natural catastrophes led to the demise of major civilizations such as the Minoans, the Mayans, and the Norse. While neighbors certainly helped neighbors across the millennia, formal, external disaster response does not seem to appear until the development of the Red Cross in the 1800s. During the Cold War, governments on both sides of the conflict strengthened their internal civilian preparations for a nuclear attack (the civil defense movement), and these efforts improved general disaster readiness. Likewise, as internationally publicized disasters struck in the 1960s and 1970s there was pressure for governments to assist their own populations efficiently, and send help to or accept aid from other nations as well.

Philippines, 2013. Photo Courtesy of Mike Morse Photography.

Following the success of the Marshall Plan, many countries created agencies focused on exporting international development philosophies and investments. A realization grew that disaster planning and response were critical elements to these efforts. Nongovernmental organizations such as the Red Cross, Oxfam, and Save the Children also developed. With all of these developments plus the rise of fast-paced international news reporting, it was no longer acceptable for catastrophes to be ignored or disregarded.

Incident Management

An important part of any successful endeavor is effective management. After World War II, the United States, like many countries, based its emergency management structure, when there was one, on military organization, with rigid ranks, divisions, and chains of communication. Catastrophic wildland fires in the 1970s in California revealed the shortcomings of this approach and the United States began developing a flexible and rapidly expandable form of emergency management that came to be called the Incident Command System (ICS). ICS has several guiding principles and establishes a standardized, but modifiable, incident management structure.

This short description of ICS is not designed to be a replacement for formal training, but here are some of the important tenets:

- Defined organizational structure: The first emergency responder or the highest ranking first responder to arrive on scene takes control of managing the incident, until someone with a more senior position reaches the event. This establishes a set chain-of-command which always expands using the same format.
- Branches and units: The ICS structure can be a small as one responder, or expand to tens of thousands, but as it expands, everyone is calling their subunits (branches and units) and leadership structure by the same names, enabling accountability and efficient information flow.
- Common nomenclature: See above.
- Expandability and contractibility: See above for expansion description, but also consider the demobilization process (getting all responders home safely when their assignment ends) from the

beginning of the event on. Return tickets, transportation, and debriefing should not be left to the last minute.

- Management by objectives: Incident managers should first consider the objectives they want to achieve (treating patients, distributing food, building shelter, etc.). This will allow them to systematically consider what resources and information they already have and what they will need to accomplish these goals.
- Span of control: For accountability, this means all supervisors should be directing, and receiving reports from no more than three to seven people. At eight or more personnel, they should consider creating subleader positions who can effectively maintain information flow, and personnel awareness.
- Integrated communications: If possible, all responders (in a zone, region, or city) should have access to the same radio frequencies, or be able to contact one command center to report findings, request resources or call for help. This hopefully ensures that one entity has a good overall picture of the disaster, rather than the dangerous and fragmented situation of teams working without coordination and support.
- Unity of command: This is easily explained by saying you only have one person giving you orders. If you have two or more people directing you, you will need clarification about who is in charge and whose orders take priority.
- Unified command system: When multiple agencies respond to an incident, representatives with the authority to make operational decisions should be communicating with each other in the command center. This is much harder to do in a large disaster, but reinforces the point that your organization should regularly check in with the local response authorities.
- Incident action plan (IAP): The IAP reflects written objectives, progress, changing conditions, completed, or additional tasks, etc. It is for a designated Operational Period, often 8, 12, or 24 hours. As the Operational Period ends, a new, updated IAP should be created for the next Operational Period. The IAP should be shared with all personnel.
- Emergency response functional roles: In the previous chapter, we discussed these 10−15 critical roles (fire suppression, public health and medical, transportation, communications, etc.).

- Command of the incident does not pass automatically to the more senior person upon arrival. They must get a briefing on current conditions, and verbally acknowledge taking command.

The ICS principles above may seem like common sense: if you are the boss, acknowledge you are taking charge of the incident; do not try to give to or receive information from too many people—you will lose track of the information and your personnel; do not assign one person to two supervisors, etc. However, these doctrines stemmed from multiple tragic incidents where, under the pressure of an emergency, poor oversight and diminished information sharing led to casualties among civilians and responders.

> **TIP**
>
> Many introductory ICS courses are available for free, on-line from Federal Emergency Management Agency (FEMA).

In addition to these principles, ICS established a management structure whose positions can be filled according to need and personnel availability. An example of a generic public health ICS position organizational chart is below, but the positions and roles are adaptable to any response focus and any disaster.

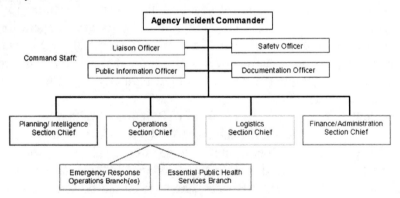

ICS is divided into courses, increasing in complexity and titled by number: ICS 100, ICS 200, etc.

The Planning P
The Planning P has become an important concept in ICS.

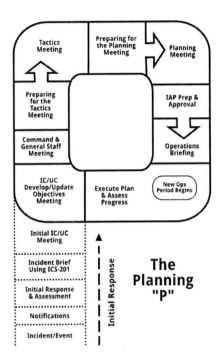

It is designed to be a reminder for members of the Planning Section of how and when they should be gathering data, developing the incident objectives, tactics, and IAP, and distributing information. I think the general lesson for everyone is that those processes should be a continuous cycle, never stopping until the incident is over.

ICS Summary
Not all disaster response organizations use ICS, and it is not necessary to use it slavishly, copying every position title and format. However, if you are on a team, and your supervisor is attempting to direct 10 people, you have two people giving you conflicting orders, you do not have written objectives or no one knows what the objectives are for the day ... do not be surprised if your group is floundering. Quickly

assess if you are operating safely and then see if you can tactfully address some of these issues.

RECOMMENDED TRAINING

For this chapter, I tried to choose more general training opportunities that any agency would appreciate. For example, even an nongovernmental organization focused on disaster food relief would appreciate having a volunteer with incident management training, first aid certification (to help their own team members in a medical emergency), and knowledge of radio communications, in addition to the specific food safety and storage, meal preparation, feeding logistics, etc., training they require.

The last chapter should have given you some ideas on the range of disaster volunteer organizations out there. Your research will have shown that each organization has at least one disaster focus, if not several. These areas of service will drive the training requirements for each group, so evaluate whether the recommendations in this chapter match up with your goals and those of your desired volunteer experience.

Community Emergency Response Team (20−80 Hours)

Many countries have encouraged municipalities to create teams of volunteer responders within each neighborhood or city. The United States calls their program the Community Emergency Response Team (CERT). In evenings and on weekends, these volunteers take several levels of training on topics such as Disaster Awareness, Fire Suppression, Disaster Medical Operations, and Light Search and Rescue. Often parts of the training can be taken on-line. The CERT team members are usually issued basic disaster response equipment such as a helmet, gloves, safety vest, and wrench to shut off leaking gas or water pipes. Teams frequently form partnerships with amateur radio operators (HAMs) or take that training themselves. In the event of a disaster, CERT members are expected to gear up and begin doing damage surveys and hazard mitigation (shutting off gas, putting out small fires, etc.) in their neighborhoods in conjunction with their local fire and police departments. The CERT training and experience is an excellent introduction to basic disaster response.

CPR/First Aid/Emergency Medical Responder/Emergency Medical or Ambulance Technician (4–200 Hours)

Even if your chosen field of disaster volunteering is not health oriented, chances are that your crew would appreciate someone with medical training in case a team member gets injured. Furthermore, a critical element of any emergency medical training, from basic cardiopulmonary resuscitation (CPR) to trauma surgeon, is keeping your head in stressful situations. This is, of course, a useful trait in disasters. Everyone should have a basic CPR course—which takes up to 4 hours and trains you on the proper response to a victim whose heart stops beating or who is choking. A valuable companion to the entry-level training is a 4–8 hour Basic First Aid course. This teaches basic emergency techniques for controlling bleeding and stabilizing fractures. These are often offered through your local Heart Association or Red Cross chapter. The next level of training is usually called Emergency Medical Responder and it lasts 48–80 hours depending on the curriculum and sponsor. It covers topics such as Legal Issues, Patient Assessment, Circulation, Medical Oxygen, and Childbirth, etc. Finally, many countries offer a 100–200 hours course called Emergency Medical Technician (EMT) or Ambulance Technician. These certifications continue the progression in medical teaching with a thorough familiarization in airway management, trauma and bleeding control, shock and allergic reactions, splinting, and so on. The EMT-level course should leave participants confident to handle almost any medical emergency with basic supplies.

As trivia and of interest to those who may visit the developing world, the symbol for emergency medical services and many other health specialties is the Rod of Asclepius. Asclepius was a Greek god associated with healing whose followers often used nonvenomous snakes in their rituals. Another connection with the serpent and the staff representation is the treatment for Guinea worms, an African parasite about the width of a piece of yarn that can infest human tissue and slowly burrow its way up and out of the skin. As the 3−4 in. (60−100 cm) "worm" gradually exits over days and weeks, the patient cannot simply pull on the parasite. It may rupture, die and cause a severe infection. Instead, the adult Guinea worm is wound around a small object like a matchstick until it eventually leaves the body completely. Thus another link between our image of snakes, sticks, and healing.

HAM (20−40 Hours)

Amateur radio operations courses are one of the mainstays of disaster response training. Established communications such as internet, phone, and fixed-antenna radio systems are often badly damaged during the incident, leaving all areas of emergency response in need of communications assistance. Satellite phones and satellite data streaming are a very expensive method of replacing these capabilities so HAM (amateur) radio will remain a critical aspect of disaster communications. The initial licensing course for HAM radio operators can take one to three 8 hour days, and there are multiple advanced courses and certifications. Entry-level radios can cost as little as $100 USD.

Food Prep/Shelter Management (1–20 Hours)

The Red Cross, among other organizations, offers detailed courses in the safe handling and preparation of food for large numbers of disaster responders and victims. Likewise, there are classes in how to safely set up temporary living quarters in gymnasiums, churches, or stadiums. These areas are surprisingly technical, with considerations for privacy, sanitation, and integrating individuals with functional needs or service animals. You may not expect to fulfill this role when you join your volunteer group, but your knowledge could fill a critical gap for your own team members or for disaster victims.

Poststorm debris, Tacloban, 2013. Photo Courtesy of Author.

Waste Management

Bulk debris management is almost always a major challenge after a disaster (see Typhoon Haiyan case study below) and there are courses available in this specialty. But, even at an individual level you should be aware of the waste you are producing (personal, medical, etc.) and how to safely dispose of it. The United Nations and the US Army offer on-line resources on the topics of postdisaster waste management: http://www.eecentre.org/Training.aspx; http://armypubs.army.mil/med/DR_pubs/dr_a/pdf/tbmed593.pdf.

Water Sanitation

Other than oxygen to breathe, there is no more critical element to human health than the provision of adequate amounts of clean water for drinking and washing. On a deployment you are responsible for your own health and you will need to be familiar with your personal water purification systems, as well as the options for and importance of handwashing and bathing. Additionally, you may find opportunities to stop the spread of diseases if you can share these messages with disaster victims. Here are several resources from the United States Center for Disease Control on various aspects of sanitation and water storage: http://www.cdc.gov/healthywater/emergency/hygiene-handwashing-diapering/index.html; http://www.ct.gov/dph/lib/dph/drinking_water/pdf/Bulk_Water_Hauling_Guidelines.pdf; http://www.who.int/water_sanitation_health/publications/2011/tn3_cleaning_disinfecting_tanks_en.pdf.

Organizational Profile

ASPCA

Used with permission: ASPCA.

Many countries have organizations dedicated to the protection of animals. For this profile we will look at the American Society for the Prevention of Cruelty to Animals (ASPCA) because they have a well-developed disaster response capability using their Field Investigations and Response (FIR) teams.

The ASPCA was founded in 1866 in New York City by Henry Bergh, a former diplomat who advocated fiercely for the interests of animals and who later went on to help found the New York Society for the Prevention of Cruelty to Children. The ASPCA was modeled after the Royal Society for the Prevention of Cruelty to Animals founded in Great Britain in 1824. Bergh and the ASPCA helped institute legal protections for animals as well

---

as innovations such as ambulances for injured draft animals, rigging devices to remove trapped animals from excavations and large animal anesthesia.

Like other organizations with disaster response capabilities, the massive animal welfare needs after Hurricane Katrina encouraged the ASPCA to expand their response and improve their partnerships with government agencies, faith-based groups, and other animal welfare responders. They now have tractor-trailer-based mobile response crews with living quarters for disaster team members, multiple treatment areas for injured animals, and hundreds of cages to safely separate their wards.

Acknowledging that many residents will not evacuate before, during, or after a disaster without knowing their animals are taken care of, in 2006 the United States passed the Pet Evacuation and Transportation Standards Act (PETS Act) which mandated that local and state emergency managers address the needs of household pets and service animals after a disaster. This continued the recognition of the importance of the animal emergency response groups like the ASPCA.

In order to be an ASPCA FIR team member, applicants must be 18 years old, and complete the following requirements:

- *ASPCA's 10 part webinar series on FIR*
- *FEMA IS100.b—Introduction to ICS*
- *IS 700—National Incident Management System, an introduction*

   Additional requirements include:

- *The ability to travel nationwide with little to no advance notice*
- *A minimum commitment of traveling 7 consecutive days*
- *High levels of flexibility and professionalism (treat animals, peers, and colleagues with care and respect)*
- *Willingness to work flexible hours, long days, and weekends*
- *Ability to work independently as well as in a team*
- *Strong interpersonal communication skills*
- *Ability to cope with physically and mentally challenging work environment*
- *Ability to create and maintain a positive and collaborative work environment*
- *May be required to complete standard background check and a motor vehicle report*

   Please note many roles may require:

- *Working with and around animals*
- *Dealing with fractious or diseased animals*
- *Exposures to zoonotic diseases (which can be transferred from animals to people)*
- *Working in extreme temperatures (hot and cold) for long periods; wearing, working, and cleaning in specific personnel protective equipment for long periods of time and/or in extreme temperatures, including but not limited to; Tyvec suits, gloves, and respirators appropriate for the specific function*

- *The ability to walk medium to long distances, which could be up to several miles including on uneven terrain*
- *The ability to stand, bend and/or kneel and reach repeatedly for long periods of time*
- *The ability to lift up to 50 pounds*

  Visit: http://aspcapro.org/how-individuals-can-participate for more information.

Disaster Case Study:

Typhoon Haiyan

On November 8, 2013, at around 5 am local time, a massive tropical cyclone named Super Typhoon Haiyan (known in the Philippines as "Yolanda") made landfall with its epicenter near city of Tacloban, in the island of Leyte, in the center of the Philippines. Haiyan was a huge storm, 300 miles/480 km across, with winds of 150–180 mph/240–290 kph. One of the most devastating aspects of the storm was an extreme storm surge of tidal waters which swept up to a mile inland with a height of 15–18 ft/ 4–6 m. Most of the estimated 6000 casualties were later found to have drowned from this rapid flooding in the early morning hours. Many residences and businesses stored large items such as bags of rice, fuel, and appliances on their first floor and once soaked, these contaminated items were a public health hazard and a debris management challenge. After the storm there were piles of rotting trash along the streets 6 ft (2 m) across, 6 ft high and up to a city block long, drawing clouds of flies as well as rats and mice.

Photo Courtesy of Author.

Tacloban was the largest city in the most affected province, with a population of 250,000, and its airport, harbor, drinking water/sanitation system, and roads were heavily damaged by the winds and flooding, hampering efforts to receive and support domestic and international relief workers. During the storm, as waters rose, local police officials let jailed prisoners free, leading to security concerns for the rest of the population. Many hospitals and other facilities had their emergency generators, X-ray, CT, computer, and other critical but heavy equipment on the first floor, where they were ruined by floodwaters. Radio antennas, cellular and landline phone services were disrupted for up to a week after the disaster, causing communications challenges.

In the first 48 hours after the storm, there were virtually no requests for assistance from Tacloban and surrounding areas. This was assumed to be a positive sign until the extent of destruction, including to the communications networks, became known. Military planes, from the Philippines and across the world, began landing at the damaged airport and assessing the needs. Advance teams scouted out areas of deployment and made contact with local representatives. Tacloban was represented by a minority political party in the Philippines and there were soon accusations that local authorities had not done enough to prepare for the storm and that the national government was withholding needed assistance for political reasons. This finger pointing is unfortunately common after major disasters.

Disaster relief workers faced many of the usual response challenges in Tacloban and surrounding areas. Housing was in short supply so some teams utilized tents for sleeping and shelter, but there was limited open and debris-free space in the city center. Many residents left Tacloban to stay with friends and family in unaffected regions of the country and some generously lent their apartments and homes to responders. Other relief workers slept in hospital rooms, churches, schools, or warehouses. The domestic water system was heavily impacted by the storm and it took several weeks to restore adequate chlorine levels to drinking water and repair damaged pipes. Relief workers were dependent on bottled water (sometimes hard to acquire) or water of unknown quality which was occasionally flowing from household taps and needed to be sanitized. Food shortages occurred as the roads, markets, farms, and ferries were all disrupted. Likewise, many families use gas to cook their meals and those canisters were soon in limited availability. The electrical grid was unreliable for an extended period of time after the storm, so radios, satellite phones, and other electronic devices had to be recharged from solar panels and generators (also in short supply, and in need of fuel). Without power, buildings were unlit at night thus headlamps and flashlights were critical.

In a storm with this massive size, in a nation made up of islands, what were the transportation challenges? On a deployment to a disaster like this, how would you charge your critical electronic equipment? Do you think the aid was evenly distributed throughout the region, or did larger cities get more and were smaller, isolated villages unintentionally ignored?

Recommended Reading

The Lassa Ward by Ross Donaldson

Dr. Ross Donaldson was still in medical school when he traveled to Africa to volunteer at a small field hospital specializing in the treatment of patients with Lassa fever, one of the deadliest diseases in the world. Upon his arrival, Donaldson had to confront isolation, austere living conditions and his fears of this highly communicable illness, which rapidly causes extreme hemorrhaging, delirium and death. At the compound, there were many patients, few supplies and a rotating cast of local and international caregivers. Sierra Leone, where the hospital was located, was in the midst of civil unrest, multiple disease outbreaks, ongoing conflicts over the hunt for blood diamonds and near famine.

After a few weeks, the director and only doctor at the Lassa hospital announced he had to leave for a several days and that he was placing Donaldson (while only a medical student, the highest trained medical provider there) in charge. Dr. Donaldson does a great job of exploring the anxiety he felt about this sudden "promotion" especially as the director's absence period lengthened from its planned duration.

This account is a vivid and compelling description of the horrific conditions suffered by patients in an underdeveloped country's public health disaster. From a personal perspective, Dr. Donaldson examining many of the uncomfortable aspects of international relief work such as trading with dubious characters for needed medicines, the effects of returning to his home country with an (initially unknown) illness and the psychological consequences of his experiences in Sierra Leone. However, the most valuable lesson I took from the book was the need for flexibility in the face of a dynamic emergency situation. As he planned his trip, Dr. Donaldson expected to function as a mid-level medical volunteer, assisting the doctor(s) and nurses at the Lassa hospital. Instead, circumstances changed and he was placed in charge of the facility while the director was traveling. This is an important reminder that we must be prepared to fulfill multiples roles in a disaster: team member, team leader, emotional supporter, and/or victim.

CHAPTER 4

Preparation and Practice

A goal without a plan is just a wish.

Antoine de Saint-Exupéry

PREPARING AND PRACTICING FOR YOUR FIRST DEPLOYMENT

Let us return to the question we have been addressing in each previous chapter: "Are you going to be an asset or a liability when you show up to help?" You have decided and you are ready to meet the physical challenges of disaster volunteering. You have got your eye on one or more potential organizations and you have picked out classes and training to better prepare you mentally.

What is next?

Unless you are going to wait for a disaster to strike your neighborhood and you plan to assist victims in your living room, it is time to leave the house.

Because you will have to travel to the scene of the catastrophe, mundane concerns like luggage, boots, travel documents, and supplies become crucial. As before, and for this chapter in particular, I encourage you to keep a journal, recording what worked for you, what did not, areas for improvement, and lists of critical items.

To explore your preparation and practice needs, please ask yourself:

- Are you an experienced and organized traveler or are you a haphazard packer, always needing to shop for forgotten items when you arrive?

- Do you have experience camping or hiking?
- Have you traveled internationally?
- Have you worked in small groups with diverse personalities to achieve tasks under pressure?
- Have you been part of a volunteer organization before?
- Are you familiar with the chain-of-command concept?
- Can you afford to take this time off?
- Will your employer, school, and family let you take this trip?

Finally, this section will introduce you to the critical concept of evaluating everything you bring from the (sometimes competing) perspectives of weight, volume, and utility. You will constantly analyze these three criteria.

TRAVELING

Well-prepared, self-sufficient travel is the foundation of being a safe, healthy, and successful disaster volunteer. If you fail to plan before you even get to your home airport, most of your energy for the rest of the trip will be spent pulling yourself together rather than helping others. For your reference, there are checklists at the end of the chapter, but the following areas are critical enough to explore in detail. The good news is that you should not have to figure this out and possibly spend a great of money on the wrong equipment the day before you leave for your first disaster deployment. Hopefully you are going to engage in systematic preparation, evaluating every part of your disaster response equipment before that day comes. My advice: Go Take a Hike.

Hiking

Hiking is excellent for developing the qualities of self-sufficiency, equipment familiarity, and mental and physical toughness that are so critical to being an effective disaster volunteer. If you are an experienced hiker, feel free to skim this section to pickup some tips on how to apply your outdoor experiences to disaster response.

If you have never hiked before, read this section and other sources of advice carefully or you will set yourself up for a miserable first experience outdoors. As earlier, you will get used to evaluating everything for its weight, volume, and utility. And, as in every area, feel free to consult hiking-focused books, articles and videos from other authors who may offer more detailed advice.

Starting from the ground up, good choices in footwear and socks are critical to your health and wellbeing. Like luggage, there are different philosophies about shoes, socks, and boots. Some people prefer to hike in light trail running shoes (as do I). For disaster response, I think it is prudent to get used to wearing more substantial footwear, with toe, ankle and heel protection. A small cut, sprain, or slip that would be inconsequential with easy access to medical care in your home town could be catastrophic or at least deployment-ending when serving in a disaster.

Go to a shoe or camping supply store and get advice from the experts on sturdy but light hiking shoes/boots. Remember the weight versus utility criteria. If you buy boots designed for climbing Mount Everest, you may be miserable in them if your disaster response duties include standing in the sun for 10−12 hours each day. Because boots are so bulky to pack, many responders wear them on the plane as they travel to assist. How will you handle 24 hours wearing them, taking them on and off for airport security, etc.?

I know medical providers who only wear running shoes on disaster deployments, because that is what they wear at their home hospital and they assume their duties and living quarters will not bring them into broken terrain. They are comfortable until they encounter deep and unavoidable puddles on the way to a location. Ditto for socks: some people recommend two pairs. Others prefer extremely thick, thin, tall, or short styles.

As you begin, I recommend a middle course, with moderate weight boots and socks. Do not spend too much money on the newest, lightest thing, remember, during a disaster you are not actually going to be hiking in these—they just need to be sturdy and comfortable and preferably on the lightweight side. But, and this is critical—get them broken in on some day hikes or wearing them around town.

Clothing will need to be chosen based on the region you expect to deploy to and the duties you hope to perform. Some disaster volunteer organizations provide a uniform, a jumpsuit/coverall, or a list of clothing expectations (khaki trousers, surgical scrubs, etc.). Lightweight, hand-washable, poly blend shirts, and pants with lots of pockets that can hang dry are most common in the disaster world. I thought the movies were portraying a cliché until I went to my first UN Health Cluster meeting in Haiti and almost every aid organization representative was actually wearing a khaki safari vest. Vests are light and can hold lots of pens, notebooks, radios, flashlights, and other supplies. Think about weight, volume, and utility-hiking will help you discover your preferences and best practices.

Health cluster meeting, Philippines, 2013. Photo Courtesy of Author.

Before you go hiking: Make a plan; consult a map; check the weather; get the right food, drink, and permits (if needed). Start with a shorter hike, especially with unfamiliar equipment. This planning experience will become critical as you expand it to.

Camping

Camping can be another great preparation tool for international disaster volunteering. This book is not intended to be a comprehensive guide, but there are many camping resources on the web, in libraries, or at your local bookstore. Some important considerations and skills to work on:

- Finding comprehensive checklists of clothing, equipment, food, and other supplies.

- Choosing appropriate luggage (backpack for hiking, suitcase for car-based camping trips, etc.).
- Smart packing (bring just what you need, being able to carry it, etc.).
- You may be purchasing a tent for use on deployment. Many volunteers bring a small, lightweight, 1–2 person tent which provides privacy, sleeping quarters, and a place to store their belongings. However, if they are provided with lodging at the disaster site this may be an item that they hauled around but is never used.
- Most volunteers bring a sleeping mat, camping pillow or pillow case, and sheets or sleeping bag. You will need to consider the expected temperature at night, weight, space available, etc.
- Do you have a quick-drying camping towel or similar?
- Evaluating how much food and water you use in 24 hours, especially while performing strenuous activities.
- Finding high energy foods that you enjoy or can at least tolerate like trail mix, electrolyte powder, freeze dried meals, and so forth.
- Reviewing what could have gone better after a hike or multiday trip: what you forgot, did not realize you would need, or brought but never used. This "closing the loop" to learn from your experiences is critical because there probably will not be any chance to acquire these items when you are serving in a disaster situation.

TIP

Do not leave batteries inside flashlights, headlamps, radios, or other electronic equipment if you are going to store the devices, unused, for more than a month or two. The batteries can leak, corrode, and ruin the equipment when you need it most.

Personal Protective Equipment

In a disaster, medical care is already limited. At all costs you want to avoid hurting yourself and diverting valuable resources. Personal protective equipment (PPE) can help you do this. This book is not designed to discuss PPE for technical search and rescue, firefighting, law enforcement, etc., which should be specified by a sponsoring organization—we will only cover general protective equipment for a disaster responder.

We have already discussed the critical importance of tough, comfortable footwear.

It is unlikely you would need a helmet unless you are doing technical rescue, but a hat can protect you from sunburn or cold temperatures as well as light scrapes and bumps in unlit areas.

Work gloves are critical for every deployment even (or especially) if you think you have a nonmanual labor assignment. In a disaster you probably will not have the luxury of people to assist you opening supply boxes, setting up equipment, rearranging and cleaning up, etc. Cuts and blisters can become infected and will decrease your effectiveness as a responder. Bring a pair of comfortable, sturdy leather, or cloth work gloves!

Goggles, sunglasses, or protective eyewear are critical, especially if you are working in a medical environment or around aircraft or high winds. Similarly for a dust protective face mask and earplugs.

Chairs, beds, and other niceties may not be usable after a disaster. If you expect to spend time on your knees treating patients, setting up equipment or cleaning up debris-consider knee pads. During the Haiti earthquake response, I spent three weeks kneeling on concrete and other hard surfaces. For the next six months I had knee pain. Now a lightweight set of knee pads come with me.

> **TIP**
>
> Bring a headlamp and spare batteries—possibly the most useful piece of gear you will have.

LUGGAGE

There are different philosophies about luggage for routine travel, let alone disaster response. Some people prefer to spend as little money as possible, knowing that the bag may rip apart at the zippers or seams after a few trips. That the suitcase needs tape and string to hold it together that last flight home is fine with them. Others buy only high end designer brands showing their exquisite taste and financial means. Some travelers like rolling bags, other want backpack straps. Hard lockable rolling case versus soft, over the shoulder duffel? Your budget and preferences will come into play, but consider these factors.

Large capacity backpack, designed for wildland firefighters—holds tent, sleeping bag, sleeping mat, clothes, and supplies for 3 days. Photo Courtesy of Author.

You may spend a lot of time in and near airport terminals with smooth floors, so wheels can save your energy. On the other hand, a disaster stricken area is, by definition, fighting to maintain infrastructure like electricity, roads, and sidewalks. You will struggle to carry heavy rolling bags the last half mile of damaged streets to your lodging up or unlit stairs with no working elevator. Hard luggage is more securable, but heavier. Expect to be transported in the back of a pickup, dump truck, or repurposed school bus with your bags crammed into every available nook, so soft-sided luggage can have an advantage.

Most volunteer organizations will ask you to limit the amount of luggage you bring (perhaps to a carry on only), to ensure they will be able to transport you safely (by air, ground, or water) to the final destination. Others will ask that you fill your checked luggage with disaster relief supplies or equipment. You will most likely want to leave your larger bag or bags in your sleeping room, while taking a daypack or fanny pack with water, food, sunscreen, and other small supplies with you to your work location each day. Can you lock it? Is this day bag your carry on or can it nest inside? Do you use a drinking water bladder system like Camelpack or Platypus to carry water throughout the day and how does that fit into your luggage?

If you bring a luxury brand suitcase worth a month of their average salaries to a poor country suffering from a disaster, is that sending a signal of empathy? Do not assume because they are poor that they would not know how much that bag costs, they have reality TV there too. Likewise, while I have never had a problem with theft while assisting others overseas, that expensive luggage may be a tempting target to someone whose tenuous livelihood was shattered by the recent catastrophe.

TIP

Plastic zip/cable ties from your local hardware store can be a light security measure, preventing someone from opening the checked bag's zippers or showing immediate evidence that it has been tampered with. Just make sure you have small, security approved scissors or nail clippers in your carry on to cut the zip tie when you arrive, or you will have tamper resisted yourself out of your own suitcase.

You probably will not have the room amenities you are used to, like a chest of drawers to unpack into, a closet with hangers, a bathroom shelf, etc. Pick a bag you can live out of when it is laying on the floor for several weeks, with lots of compartments and organizational capacity.

What will the volunteer organization need and which philosophy are you pursuing with your checked luggage? Collapsible duffels that can be rolled up and brought home? Hard-cased containers to protect important equipment and supplies? A couple of throwaway bags you picked up at the thrift store or your parents' attic the day before? The last option is not a great one. The community will be struggling to manage thousands of tons of debris left after the disaster. You are not doing them any favors by leaving decrepit suitcases to be disposed of. Ditto for your old T-shirts, worn out running shoes, and broken alarm clock—take them back home when you leave or do not bring them.

Big concepts to think about—are you getting a sturdy, quality bag with carry on capability and lots of internal and external pockets and compartments? Will it roll with large wheels or be carried comfortably for extended distances with padded straps or both? If you have checked luggage, can you "mate" them with your carry on or daypack so you can pull or lift the entire collection easily, leaving one hand to hold on to the side of a pickup truck, helicopter, or boat? Is the luggage rain, stain, abuse, and pilfer resistant? Are there hooks, straps, and clips for your hat, water bottle, and other needed supplies?

TENTS AND MOSQUITO PROTECTION

Depending on the host location, you may have a building to stay in during your deployment. Your volunteer organization may send your group with large multiperson tents. Or, you may need to provide your own. You should have tried them out before this! You should definitely check them twice before you deploy! I had carefully chosen a lightweight but sturdy and well ventilated unit appropriate for deployment to warm environments. I was camping in the United States when the 2015 Nepal earthquake struck. In the pouring rain, a friend helped disassemble my deployment tent and a larger one I had loaned her. In the rush to leave, the poles got switched for the two tents and when I arrived in Kathmandu I realized my tent was useless. Luckily our group had brought larger ones—but I hauled that equipment around the world and back for no reason.

If you are volunteering in an area with mosquitos, you should bring mosquito netting to sleep under. You can buy the smallest, most easily packable unit which will tuck under the edges of your sleeping mat or mattress and narrows to a point above you. Or you can buy a larger unit that gives you more room to maneuver. Bring cord and some hooks to hang this from the ceiling or a light fixture. Be aware that if your hand, foot, or head comes to rest against the netting during the night, insects can and will land on the fabric and bite you. Larger netting units have an internal frame which holds the cloth away from you, preventing this, but they are bulkier. In some countries you can buy mosquito netting treated with insect repellent, in others it is not available. Lastly, there are some free standing antibug "huts" which look like small tents made completely out of mesh. You unzip a door panel to enter and exit. These have the advantage of more internal space and no need for hooks or cords to hang from ceilings or walls, but again take slightly more space in your luggage and on the floor of the sleeping room. Whichever unit you decide on, try it beforehand so you know what accessories it needs and how to set it up.

Some Notes on Snivel Gear

"Snivel gear" is a military term for small luxuries that greatly improve your life when you are in an uncomfortable/austere living situation. Over the course of many years I have discovered a list of things that make me feel much better when I am deployed overseas at a disaster. I share them with you despite my possible embarrassment.

- Lip balm/sunscreen
- Nail clippers/tweezers
- Earplugs
- Eye shade
- Tea bags
- Instant oatmeal
- Flip-flop sandals
- Clothes pins/clothesline
- Nutrition bars/electrolyte powder
- Music device/headphones
- Plastic zip ties
- Shorts to sleep in
- A notebook and waterproof marker
- A multitool with knife, pliers, etc. (must go in checked luggage).

Each of the above items comes from a negative personal experience. I find it harder to focus on helping others when my lips are severely chapped or I am sunburned. Ditto for long, ragged nails. You will probably be sharing sleeping quarters with multiple people, some of whom will snore, or talk, or be on a different work shift altogether—earplugs, eye shades, and headphones are critical. You may be sharing accommodations with all genders, ages, and convictions-do not expect to sleep in your underwear, even if it is stifling hot. Bring something comfortable but modest to relax in after your shift or to sleep in. Tea and instant oatmeal packets are light—but boiled water is usually available and they provide me with a warm morale boost when starting a busy day on deployment. Plastic zip/cable ties have become my construction material of choice for any number of makeshift creations and fixes—I.V. bag holders, shoe laces, curtain rings, luggage handles, etc. Finally, I have learned the hard way that while working and sweating in the heat, I am prone to incapacitating muscle cramps if I only rehydrate with water. I now bring electrolyte powder with me.

Some international organizations expect each of their volunteers to bring a lightweight tent and sleeping mat. This solves the privacy issues but will add weight and volume to your luggage. No need to buy all of this at the beginning. Rent or borrow these items until you figure out what you like or what you think you will need.

If you have a specific disaster role in mind, such a medical volunteer, construction, or communications, see how well you travel or hike with the minimum (air travel allowed) tools (like stethoscope, tape measure, radio set, etc.) for your duties.

In the expedition checklists at the end of this chapter you will see some very pricey and specialized equipment like satellite phones, emergency beacons, and two way radios. Your organization should be providing items like these, if needed at all. Purchase them only if you are a gadget buff, have disposable income and like to carry extra weight around.

Head out on that camping trip. Challenge yourself but have fun. Go solo to see how you handle being alone for 2−3 days. Go with a group of friends to see how everyone (including you) handles dividing tasks, unpacking, cleanup, and the other duties. How did your luggage do? Weight, volume, and utility? Your checklists, your packing, your foot-wear, and your food? Take notes, make improvements—repeat.

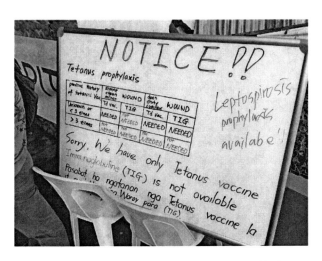

Notification of available vaccines—Tacloban, Philippines, 2013. Photo Courtesy of Author.

Financial and Personal Implications

Can you afford the luggage, equipment, vaccinations, training, passport, airfare, and other travel costs? Create a checklist, make a budget. Research best prices on equipment, and what immunizations your insurance will cover. Start saving now for that expensive international ticket, mosquito net, solar charger, or critical piece of snivel gear.

TIP

Set aside several thousand dollars (or the equivalent in your currency) for your equipment costs and a last-minute plane ticket to the disaster site.

SUMMING UP

We have covered a lot in this chapter: useful equipment, experiences, leadership, financial, and personal preparedness. Finally, I would encourage you to seek out a mentor. When you do find an organization to join, tactfully ask one of the more experienced members for 15 or 20 minutes of their time to convey the lessons they have learned from past deployments. Most are happy to give their advice (our families are sick of these war stories).

Organizational Profile

United States Disaster Medical Assistance Teams

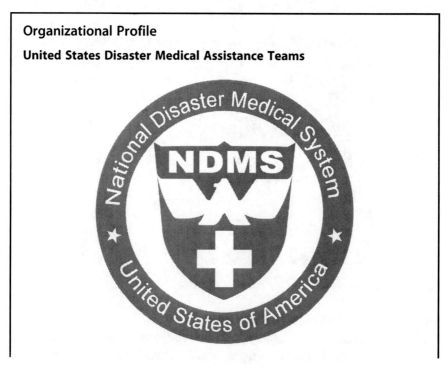

Functioning under the United States' federal Department of Health and Human Services (HHS) Assistant Secretary for Preparedness and Response (ASPR), there are approximately 80 United States Disaster Medical Assistance Teams (DMAT) teams across the country. Each team has approximately 45–70 members, the majority of whom are medical providers such as doctors, nurses, physician's assistants, respiratory therapists, paramedics, and emergency medical technicians. The federal government provides uniforms, medical equipment, patient treatment and team housing tents, food, water, fuel, and transportation for the providers during a disaster. There are slots on each team reserved for nonmedical positions such as logistics and communications.

The DMAT concept originated in the 1980s. The federal government encouraged local medical providers who wished to volunteer after a disaster to come up with an organized team concept and standardized equipment and capabilities. DMAT members deploy in configurations of 60, 45, or 30 members, expected to staff a field emergency treatment area for 72 hours without being resupplied. Team members are expected to attend local monthly or quarterly meetings as volunteers, but are considered and paid as intermittent federal employees during an actual deployment. Each team is on call 2 months a year as first-up to be called, and 1 month a year backing up the primary teams. DMAT members have been sent to the 2012 Haiti earthquake, Hurricanes Katrina, Ike, Gustav, and Sandy as well as large planned events such as presidential inaugurations. Their primary focus is on domestic disaster missions, but they occasionally deploy overseas.

The good news is that any DMAT deployment has dozens or even hundreds of experienced disaster responders and millions of federal dollars in tents, trucks, satellite communications, portable lab, and cardiology, water purification, etc., in support. However, there are a lot of teams, and they are all hoping for an order from the feds to deploy. The teams are expensive, so they only go to major (mostly domestic) disasters. Many teams only go to one or two of these incidents a decade. If a rapid deployment pace is your goal, they are not probably the right organization for you.

Finally, like any government bureaucracy, it can be difficult to get "hired" on a DMAT team, even as a semivolunteer. You must be an American citizen with a clean criminal background, financial stability, and professional references. They only accept applications (a lengthy electronic form) when there are team vacancies (listed on usajobs.gov) for specific operational roles. The job descriptions are regularly evaluated and rewritten, and the hiring is frozen for months or years during those revisions. The hiring process and background check often take a year or more.

If you are interested, do a web search for the nearest teams. Each one has a unique identifier linked to their state of origin such as CA-1

(California team #1) or FL-3 (Florida #3). Most have their own websites. Make contact with one of the team administrators. Explain your strengths and interests. Ask to attend a meeting so they can get to know you. If it is a good fit, they will walk you through the rest of the process.

Hiking/Camping checklist

The 10 essentials
    by REI
    For safety, survival, and basic comfort: (be careful of what can/cannot be brought aboard planes in carry-on/checked luggage)

1. *Navigation*
    a. *Map (with protective case)*
    b. *Compass*
    c. *GPS (optional)*
    d. *Altimeter (optional)*
2. *Sun protection*
    a. *Sunscreen*
    b. *Lip balm*
    c. *Sunglasses*
3. *Insulation*
    a. *Jacket, vest, pants, gloves, hat (see Clothing, below)*
4. *Illumination*
    a. *Headlamp or flashlight*
    b. *Extra batteries*
5. *First-aid supplies*
    a. *First-aid kit*
6. *Fire*
    a. *Matches or lighter*
    b. *Waterproof container*
    c. *Fire starter (for emergency survival fire)*
7. *Repair kit and tools*
    a. *Knife or multitool*
    b. *Repair kits for stove, mattress; duct tape strips*
8. *Nutrition*
    a. *Extra day's supply of food*
9. *Hydration*
    a. *Water bottles or hydration reservoirs*
    b. *Water filter or other treatment system*
10. *Emergency shelter*
    a. *Tent, tarp, bivy, or reflective blanket*

Beyond the 10 essentials

- *Backpack*
- *Daypack or summit pack*
- *Pack cover*
- *Tent, tarp, or bivy sack (with stakes, guylines)*
- *Tent-pole repair sleeve*
- *Footprint (if desired for tent)*
- *Sleeping bag*
- *Stuff sack or compression sack*
- *Sleeping pad*
- *Pillow or stuffable pillow case*
- *Whistle (plus signaling mirror)*
- *Multifunction watch with altimeter*
- *Trekking poles*
- *Meals*
- *Energy food (bars, gels, chews, trail mix)*
- *Energy beverages or drink mixes*
- *Stove*
- *Fuel*
- *Cookset (with pot grabber)*
- *Dishes or bowls*
- *Utensils*
- *Cups (measuring cups)*
- *Bear canister (or hang bags for food)*
- *Nylon cord (50' for hanging food)*
- *Backup water treatment*
- *Collapsible sink or container*
- *Packable lantern*

Clothing: Warm weather

- *Wicking T-shirt (synthetic or wool)*
- *Wicking underwear*
- *Quick-drying pants or shorts*
- *Long-sleeve shirt (for sun, bugs)*
- *Sun-shielding hat*
- *Bandana or Buff*

Clothing: Cool weather

- *Wicking long-sleeve T-shirt*
- *Wicking long underwear (good sleepwear)*
- *Hat, cap, skullcap, balaclava, or headband*
- *Gloves or mittens*
- *Rainwear (jacket, pants)*
- *Fleece jacket or vest, and pants*

Footwear; assorted personal items

- *Hiking boots or hiking shoes suited to terrain*
- *Socks (synthetic or wool) plus spares*
- *Gaiters*
- *Sandals (for fording, in camp)*
- *Camera*
- *Extra memory cards*
- *Binoculars*
- *Permits*
- *Route description or guidebook*
- *Field guide(s); star identifier*
- *Outdoor journal and pen or pencil*
- *Credit card; small amount of cash*
- *Earplugs and eye shade*
- *Toilet paper*
- *Sanitation trowel*
- *Hand sanitizer*
- *Insect repellent*
- *Bear spray*
- *Toothbrush and/or toiletry kit*
- *Biodegradable soap (and shower bag)*
- *Quick-dry towel*
- *Cell phone/satellite communicator/2-way radios*
- *Personal locator beacon*
- *Posthike snacks, water, towel, and clothing change*
- *Trip itinerary left with friend and under car seat*

CHAPTER 5

Predeployment Preparations

Man cannot discover new oceans unless he has the courage to lose sight of the shore.

Andre Gide

INTRODUCTION

This point of your preparation to become a disaster volunteer is like the first long uphill pull when riding a roller coaster but you cannot quite yet tell where the ride will take you. You waited a long time for this. You are excited and a little bit scared. You still have time to prepare, and you should use it wisely, but very soon the extreme ups and downs of an actual deployment will begin.

Physical Fitness

All the supplies and knowledge in the world will not help you if you are unable to physically accomplish tasks in a disaster (locally or internationally). There is no preferred body type, age, or gender to be a successful disaster volunteer. However, an effective team member will have the strength and stamina to travel in cramped conditions for hours or days, then do heavy manual labor to set up relief efforts, then work long hours performing their mission without air conditioning or other comforts, all while getting little sleep and limited nutrition.

If you have not recently, see a physician for a check-up and evaluation. Take an honest look at your capabilities and medical needs. If you are in fragile health, a disaster zone will only exacerbate your conditions, and you will end up taking medical care away from the local victims.

How to Become an International Disaster Volunteer.

Photo Courtesy of Mike Morse Photography.

In preparation to become a disaster volunteer and with your physician's input, create a plan to address your fitness weaknesses. Any type of physical activity is better than nothing but your results will be commensurate with your efforts. A program of ballroom dancing will increase your cardiovascular fitness, leg/core strength, and nimbleness, but if you are asked to spend several days in a disaster zone moving heavy boxes to and from high shelves, you may wish you had done more upper body exercises as well. Because of this, I recommend you incorporate elements of "functional fitness" into your workout program. The root of this philosophy is a goal that you will be able to do daily activities more easily by increasing your capacity to move your own bodyweight through a variety of situations, including jumping, climbing, squatting, crawling, etc. And that you are also reasonably prepared to lift heavy objects you may encounter. Please consider that your daily activities during a disaster will be a great deal harder than those in your "normal" life.

Many of these functional fitness programs, such as crossfit and "boot camp" experiences, incorporate calisthenics (like push-ups and pull-ups) and other simple movements done rapidly one after another to increase your strength and cardiovascular endurance and the trainers may add weightlifting to increase capacity past your bodyweight. To begin, you can go to a gym, join classes or hire a personal trainer. If your time, money, or access is limited, there are free on-line exercise schedules and instructional videos or you can find resources at your local library. Whatever you do, do something—even a few months of sustained effort will help. Do not take your physical fitness for granted or you will find it will let you, and your team, and the people you have come to help down at the worst possible time.

INTERNATIONAL TRAVEL

Not surprisingly, another good preparation tool for international disaster volunteering is international travel, especially if you do not have a lot of experience in this area. Making a travel plan, getting your documents in order, and navigating airports, customs and taxis in another language will make you that much more comfortable when you have to do this on short notice for an international disaster.

Before you travel, get used to gathering background information from international and local news sources, maps/guidebooks, your state department advisories, and travel blogs. Michelin sells respected paper road maps which can be useful if your phone navigation applications are not working. The Lonely Planet travel guides are excellent, detailed sources of information and their companion web blog/board provides a venue for travelers to post updates and recommendations between book editions.

From your research, are there elections scheduled, terrorist threats, epidemics, protests, strikes, holidays, or upcoming sports championships which may affect your trip? The organization which sponsors your international disaster volunteering may provide a briefing when you go, or they may not. It is better to be accustomed to quickly gathering this information on your own.

Once you are there, stay in a hostel, take public transportation, try the local delicacies (carefully), and rub elbows with people from many different backgrounds. Put the planning and packing skills (and equipment) you have been gathering for hiking and camping to the test. Please be culturally aware of your surroundings—is that T-shirt with the profanity on it a good fit for a conservative country? Are clothes that expose your shoulders, stomach, or legs going to offend the locals with whom you are interacting?

Photo Courtesy of Mike Morse Photography.

Keep notes—what worked and what did not? What stressed you out? What comforted you? Most of all, enjoy the experience. Spoiler alert—I am going to ask you to keep this same positive attitude even when you are deployed to a real disaster.

Finally, when you do travel, go easy on yourself. You will forget something, or you will bring something unneeded-journal it and make changes when you get home.

INSURANCE, DOCUMENTS, PHONE, MEDICAL CONCERNS

Many international volunteer organizations require their team members to purchase emergency medical treatment/evacuation insurance or they automatically provide it. Even if it is not required, I strongly recommend investigating the costs and terms of a policy from a reputable company for any trip to an underdeveloped area whether for a disaster, routine volunteer work, or tourism. You can add the insurance provider's contact information and that estimated cost to your personal predeployment checklist.

It is your responsibility to ensure that your travel documents are up to date. Many countries will not allow you to enter unless your passport will be valid for at least more 6 months. I had been meaning to renew my passport when a typhoon struck the Philippines and I was asked to deploy on short notice. I bought my ticket, arrived at the airport, met my deployment team and discovered that my passport would expire in five and a half months. I could not board the flight. This was a major issue and a waiver from Manila did not come through until a few minutes before my departure. That was stressful and could have been hurt the team as well as wasted my time, effort, and money.

Likewise, you will need to find out about visas and/or proof of financial self-sufficiency, i.e., showing evidence of a specific amount of money in one of your bank accounts. Get used to researching these items before an incident so you will know where to find this information. During a disaster, visa requirements may be waived. Or they may not. Those foreign currency visa payments may be a critical part of a poorer country's budget.

> **TIP**
>
> If you plan to use your mobile phone during an international disaster (if there is service) or an international trip, make sure it will function in that region and be aware of any roaming charges for data, calls, or texts. Is it recommended that you purchase a new SIM card for that country and will your model telephone accept those? Do you have the right international adapter for your power charger, etc.?

Finally, while it is highly unlikely that anything fatal will happen to you, I recommend that you have, at the minimum, a simple last will and testament. This will spare your loved ones the stress of trying to guess your intentions while dealing with many other emotions and obligations.

Medical Issues

Different regions of the world have requirements and/or recommendations for specific immunizations such as yellow fever, dengue, or medicines like doxycycline you would need to take while in country to prevent malaria. It would be impossible to predict exactly where the disaster will occur to which you will deploy. However, there are standard vaccinations everyone with high risk duties should have like tetanus, diphtheria, pertussis, hepatitis, and in some countries tuberculosis. Research the common shots needed for areas such as South America, Asia, and Africa. Speak to a travel physician. If you need out-of-the-ordinary vaccinations, would your doctor have access to them or is there a travel clinic in your city where you can get them? How much would they cost? Another advantage to international traveling before the disaster strikes is that you have these immunizations completed and you can try out some of the preventative medications before you are deployed.

Years ago, on a sightseeing trip to Africa, I took an antimalaria prescription which the pharmacist warned might cause me unsettling dreams. Unsettling dreams was a major understatement. Each night sleeping felt like 8 hours of grueling psychotherapy where exes, family members, bosses, and teachers lined up in my head to confront me on my shortcomings and failures. I woke up every morning emotionally exhausted and depressed. When I returned, a little investigation showed that many people taking this medication had the same negative side effects and that there were alternative drugs to prevent malaria available. On subsequent trips to malaria-prone regions, I used the alternatives. Do your research on side effects before you leave.

You may have existing medical conditions like diabetes, seizures, or high blood pressure. Routine international trips are a great way to see how you cope with long hours, strange foods, and new sleeping routines. Do you have enough of your medications with you? What would happen if you lost one of your pill bottles? Could you get a replacement prescription? Could you explain your medical situation to a local doctor if they did not speak your language well, or did not speak it at all?(see the First-Aid Checklist).

Licenses and Certifications

Hopefully, you are bringing not only your enthusiasm to international disaster volunteering, but also a specific skill such as medical, construction/engineering, food service, communications expertise, etc. Make sure that you travel with the originals and copies of all of your licensure cards, certificates, and important professional documents. Have any expired? Did you search out the licensing body that was international or best known in that field, if there is more than one?

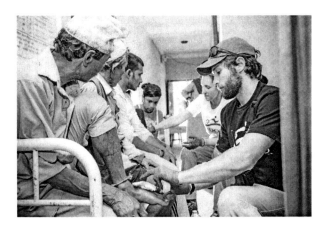

Photo Courtesy of Mike Morse Photography.

SMALL GROUP OPERATIONS AND VOLUNTEERING

I hinted at the importance of small group dynamics when I talked about camping with your friends, but the psychology of working with others under stress is critical. You probably learned many of these lessons as a child playing on a sports team, in class, as a boy or girl scout, or in a school club or church group. Remember that exasperating person you could not stand to be around for an hour? Imagine being deployed with them to live and work together 24 hours a day for several weeks. (I am sure that annoying person was not you or me.) These interpersonal issues can be magnified in a volunteer setting if some participants feel they deserve special treatment because they are not getting paid.

Now is the time to learn what bothers you and how to manage those emotions. May be your disaster volunteer organization has a local chapter and ongoing duties. Sign up. If not, look for other opportunities. Build a house. Feed the homeless. Help an animal shelter. Read to children. You may find you are the youngest volunteer or the oldest. You may dislike the loud, bossy worker next to you or love their forcefulness.

You may feel uncomfortable, out of place, ill-prepared and stressed. This is good. You will be sleeping in your own bed tonight so let these experiences be a low intensity inoculation to the anxiety you will experience on your first deployment.

I cannot stress enough how important knowing yourself and your emotional responses will be, and maintaining psychological resiliency and flexibility when faced with stress and unpleasant circumstances. Chapter 6, Psychological Readiness, goes into these preparations in detail but here is a real world example.

A good friend and experienced international medical relief worker was recently deployed by a respected international volunteer organization with a team to assist patients suffering from Ebola in West Africa. The group was crammed with highly educated professionals with little disaster experience. As soon as they arrived in country, several members reacted to the stress by shutting themselves in their rooms and refusing to come out. When the patient load dwindled and the medical volunteers were asked to shift roles and gather data, several refused, saying that work was beneath them. Other team members ignored safety guidelines, feeling that their judgment should take precedence over established procedures. They decided to sightsee and mingle with the local population, needlessly exposing themselves to the virus. Obviously, this deployment was a failure: putting the team and patients at risk; leaving the community needs unmet, the organization with a bad reputation, and the volunteers with a negative and unfulfilling experience.

Do not be part of the problem—learn how not to be that needy, ineffective, immature volunteer, and learn how to calmly, positively and productively deal with the team member who is overwhelmed by what they are experiencing.

Leadership and Management

The previous section alluded to managing difficult team members. It is highly unlikely you will be assuming a leadership role on your first disaster deployment(s). (However, it is not impossible. See Dr. Ross Donaldson's excellent memoir "Life on the Lassa Ward.") The most valuable leadership role you can play is by being a good team member. Be mentally, emotionally, and physically prepared to do whatever it takes to complete the mission, without complaining, gossiping, second-guessing, or malingering. Do it, do it cheerfully, smile when the day is done, then get up and do it again.

We talked in Chapter 3, Developing Relevant Training and Education for Deployments, about the Incident Command System, which provides valuable leadership and management training. However, nothing in real life is as black and white as those courses, so do not expect your fellow volunteers to follow those principles or even be aware of them.

If you are interested in exploring a leadership role, start in your home country, not with a team of virtual strangers during a disaster. Work with a local volunteer group as mentioned above and gain familiarity with how to manage volunteers in day-to-day life. Feel free to read motivational literature and study the methods and speeches of respected generals and CEOs. But, I have found the most effective leaders set an example by working hard, having fun, praising often, and listening well.

Ocean rescue volunteers wait for Syrian refugees in Greek waters. Photo Courtesy of Mike Morse Photography.

Recommended Reading

A Paradise Built in Hell: The Extraordinary Communities that Arise in Disaster

Rebecca Solnit

Ms. Solnit is an established writer and activist whose positive personal experiences following the 1989 Loma Prieta, California earthquake ran counter to the established narrative that humans will revert to a primitive, brutal, and selfish state following a disaster. The overwhelming majority of what she observed occurring after this major earthquake (63 deaths, 3700 injuries, $6 billion USD damages) were individuals generously assisting fellow residents, visitors, and strangers, rather than indulging in violence, theft, and chaos. Later, her research showed this to be true for other affected areas in Northern California, not just her neighborhood. Solnit, a historian, was intrigued and went back to analyze other major disasters to see if this altruism was a trend or an aberration.

She found that immediately following the 1906 San Francisco Earthquake (approximately 3000 deaths) in the same region, poor victims spontaneously organized to distribute scarce food, water, and other needed supplies to the vulnerable among their neighbors: women, children, and the elderly. These relief efforts crossed racial and class boundaries at the time, such as the separation of "white" Americans and the many Chinese laborers living in the bay area. In her second major conclusion, Ms. Solnit posits that the local wealthy elite, who needed to keep the underclasses hostile and divided against each other to decrease labor costs and organization, downplayed reports of cooperation and charity while exaggerating accounts of looting and violence. They established a public storyline of postdisaster brutality, theft and selfishness which justified calling in the military to reestablish "order" and the status quo. Ms. Solnit's conclusions are provocative and often focus on the class antagonism she observes simmering below many of our daily activities.

Ms. Solnit goes on to research and analyze similar patterns of spontaneous cooperation and charity as well as political/cultural exploitation following other major disasters like the Halifax ship explosion of 1917 (2000 deaths, 9000 injured), the 1985 Mexico City earthquake (possibly 10,000 deaths, 10,000 injured), the 2001 New York terror attack (3000 deaths, 6000 injured), and Hurricane Katrina (1800 deaths) in 2006.

There is a saying in the modern news business that "if it bleeds, it leads." In other words, the media often tends to focus on the shocking, controversial and divisive. For example, we saw stories of mass looting, rape, and murder by certain ethnic and socioeconomic groups in New Orleans after Hurricane Katrina but very few were later substantiated. This seems to lend credence to Ms. Solnit's theories.

As a disaster responder, and an optimistic human being, it was encouraging for me to read the many positive examples of generosity and unplanned charity that Solnit finds after these horrific events, but disappointing that she uncovers so many instances of sensationalized and biased reporting, which appear to assist certain privileged populations as they scramble to maintain their position in society.

Whether you ultimately agree with her optimism for human nature following a disaster and/or her criticism of the powerful and their supporters, Ms. Solnit's book is highly readable, thoroughly researched and makes it clear that the aftermath of a catastrophe is a complicated and contentious place, not just physically, but culturally and politically as well.

Case Study:

Nepal Earthquake

At approximately noon local time on Saturday morning, April 25, 2015 a magnitude 7.8 earthquake struck the country of Nepal causing 8000 deaths and 21,000 injuries. Nepal was one of the poorest countries in Asia even before this catastrophe and the emergency response was hampered by political instability and lack of infrastructure. The nation sustained an estimated 10 billion USD in damage, nearly 50% of their gross domestic product.

Although the seismic risks of the region had been well documented historically, due to poverty and lack of alternative building materials, most buildings in Nepal (especially in rural areas) are constructed of unreinforced masonry: blocks of stone and concrete held together by mortar. This type of construction is especially vulnerable to collapse following earthquakes. Experts believe that the death toll would have been much higher had the event happened at night, but many rural inhabitants were working in the fields at the time the quake struck. Conversely, some other groups were disproportionately impacted. Many Nepalese Christians worship on Saturday mornings and were trapped or killed in their churches. Similarly, several historical temples which were popular tourist attractions collapsed, killing foreign and local visitors, guides, and workers.

There were multiple aftershocks in the days and weeks following the earthquake which caused additional injuries, deaths, and damages. Those shocks interrupted rescue and relief efforts and further traumatized the population already unsettled by the initial quake. The international airport, cellular phone service, and other critical elements of the infrastructure were intermittently shut down by these events. A second major (magnitude 7.3) earthquake struck on the afternoon of May 12, causing 150 more deaths and 2500 more injuries.

The Nepalese military managed the response and relief efforts with eventual assistance from the United Nations. Dozens of international rescue and medical teams flooded Kathmandu, the capital, and local authorities struggled at times to coordinate their efforts. International teams were still en route a week later when the national government declared they had sufficient response resources and began denying entry to foreign groups. This decision was debatable but understandable as survivability was unlikely 7 or more days after the incident and the existing teams were competing for food, water, transportation, and areas to operate in. Similarly, experienced rescue task forces had begun to demobilize and give their medical supplies to local providers when the second major aftershock struck, leaving them scrambling to respond. It is easy to second guess these decisions following a disaster, but no course of action will ever be one hundred percent correct.

Nepalese children building play "shelters" to imitate their parents' efforts. Photo Courtesy of Author.

After the first quake, farmers in particular struggled because they had already entered the short time period to bring in crops ready for harvest or watch them spoil and face financial devastation. They had to try to rebuild their damaged homes in the mornings or evenings around this obligation. Many village schools were destroyed, leaving children in these communities with little to do each day if they were not helping with the harvest. Reestablishing a routine is important for kids affected by a catastrophe and it was difficult for this to happen. As in most other disasters, there were political concerns. Nepal shares borders with China and India (traditional rivals), both of which sent aid but there were reports that foreign military helicopters bringing assistance and personnel were asked to avoid the margins of Nepalese territory approaching China, for example. Lastly, major incidents like this often open the door for further exploitation of at risk groups like women and children. For years, Nepal has battled human trafficking for prostitution and labor and the economic damage following the earthquake(s) only increased these vulnerabilities.

First-Aid Checklist (Courtesy of the United States Center for Disease Control)

Medicines
Special Note About Prescription Medicines
- Pack your prescription medications in your carry-on luggage
- Pack copies of all prescriptions, including the generic names for medications
- Pack a note on letterhead stationery from the prescribing physician for controlled substances and injectable medications
- Leave a copy of your prescriptions at home with a friend or relative
- Check with the Embassy or Consulate to make sure that your medicines will be allowed into the country you are visiting. Some countries do not let visitors bring certain medicines into the country
- Prescription medicines you usually take
  - If you have a severe allergy and epinephrine has been prescribed by your doctor, bring your epinephrine autoinjector (e.g., an EpiPen)
- Special prescriptions for the trip
  - Medicines to prevent malaria, if needed
  - Antibiotic prescribed by your doctor for self-treatment of moderate to severe diarrhea
- Over-the-counter medicines
  - Antidiarrheal medication (e.g., bismuth subsalicylate, loperamide)
  - Antihistamine
  - Decongestant, alone or in combination with antihistamine
  - Antimotion sickness medication
  - Medicine for pain or fever (such as acetaminophen, aspirin, or ibuprofen)
  - Mild laxative
  - Cough suppressant/expectorant
  - Cough drops
  - Antacid
  - Antifungal and antibacterial ointments or creams
  - 1% hydrocortisone cream

Other Items That May Be Useful in Certain Circumstances
- Supplies to prevent illness or injury
  - Insect repellent containing DEET (30–50%) or picaridin (up to 15%)
  - Sunscreen (preferably SPF 15 or greater) that has both UVA and UVB protection
  - Antibacterial hand wipes or alcohol-based hand sanitizer containing at least 60% alcohol
  - Lubricating eye drops
- First-aid supplies
  - First-aid quick reference card
  - Basic first-aid items (bandages, gauze, ace bandage, antiseptic, tweezers, antibiotic ointment, scissors, and cotton-tipped applicators)
  - Moleskin for blisters
  - Aloe gel for sunburns
  - Digital thermometer
  - Oral rehydration solution packets
- Health insurance card (either your regular plan or supplemental travel health insurance plan) and copies of claim forms
- Mild sedative or other sleep aid
- Medicine to prevent altitude sickness
- Water purification tablets

CHAPTER 6

Psychological Readiness

It isn't stress that makes us fall—it's how we respond to stressful events.

Wayde Goodall

In Chapter 5, Predeployment Preparations, we discussed the importance of getting physically fit and having the right vaccinations and medications for your deployment. It is just as critical and perhaps more so that you are psychologically ready and resilient for the challenges you are about to face.

As you did with your physical condition, take stock of your mental health. Have you experienced severe depression or other significant psychological issues in the past or are you currently? What is your history of traumatic stress? Have you discussed your disaster volunteering plans with your caregiver, a family member, a spiritual advisor, or someone who is familiar with your condition? Is your family prepared for your deployment? Do they agree with you that you are ready for this potentially highly stressful situation and being away?

I will warn you that disaster volunteering is an emotional roller coaster, both on and after a deployment. The first few days during an incident, I feel "high" from the adrenalin of travel, responding and the excitement of a new situation. Afterwards, I inevitably feel a multiday "crash" when I realize how much work there is to be done to help the victims, fueled by exhaustion and overstimulation, and often exacerbated by team dynamics and different personalities. After that low, my spirits come back up. I come to terms with the heavy work load. By then fatigue is making me sleep better despite the new/uncomfortable arrangements. And I begin to appreciate the positive attributes of my fellow team members.

How to Become an International Disaster Volunteer.

The same roller coaster repeats itself upon my return home. For a few days or a week or two, I'm happy to reconnect with loved ones as well as have hot water, electricity, and tasty meals. But quickly I become disillusioned with the mundane chores of daily "normal" life—missing the excitement of the disaster zone and the intense teamwork with the same people I had been complaining about. That eventually mellows out to an acceptance of my regular existence as well as positive memories from the response.

Please take the time to evaluate your mental fitness to respond before you exacerbate existing conditions and become a burden to your team rather than an asset to the victims.

Dr. Merritt Schreiber, a psychologist who specializes in disasters and trauma at the University of California—Los Angeles David Geffen School of Medicine has created an important behavioral health system for disaster responders called "Anticipate, Plan, and Deter." You can consider this a form of immunization or mental health Personal Protective Equipment for the demanding and often negative psychological experiences you may endure on your deployment.

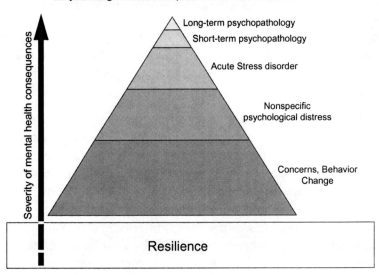

Psychological consequences of disasters

MENTAL RESILIENCY—ANTICIPATE, PLAN, DETER

Disaster responders are at high risk for posttraumatic stress and other adverse mental health consequences. If unaddressed, those effects can last a lifetime and damage your relationships, career, and academic endeavors. I cannot emphasize enough the importance of dealing with your psychological health before, during and after your volunteer commitment. Dr. Schreiber has developed the PsySTART Responder Self-Triage system. This is an overview of his precepts, which were created to assist medical workers in a disaster, but I believe have great value for disaster volunteers of all types.

Step One: ANTICIPATE
First, Dr. Schreiber recommends understanding and anticipating what might directly cause "Traumatic Response Stress" during a response. These triggers are part of the PsySTART Responder Triage system and include:

- Witnessing extreme wounds such as severe burns, dismemberment, or mutilation.
- Seeing pediatric deaths or severe injuries.
- An unusually high number of deaths different than your experience with death so far.
- The responsibility to medically triage (prioritize for treatment) patients who were expected to die to allocate limited medical resources ethically.
- If you felt that your life was in danger.
- You were injured or became ill.
- You saw the injury, death or serious illness of a fellow volunteer.

There also nontraumatic stressors which need to be managed as they can trigger "Cumulative Response Stress" which builds on past memories, experiences, or loss. These can include:

- Victims screaming in pain/fear
- Having to abandon disaster victims
- Inability to meet victims' needs or having to decrease what service/resource they would optimally receive
- Direct contact with grieving family members
- Requested to perform duties outside of current skills

- Hazardous working conditions (such as extreme shift length, compromised site safety or security or lack of personal protective equipment)
- Unable to return home as scheduled
- Worried about safety of family members, significant others or pets
- Unable to communicate with family members or significant others
- Health concerns for self-due to agent/toxic exposure (infectious disease, chemical, radiological, etc.)

You should anticipate your possible reactions to disaster stress:

- Emotional: irritability, anger, sadness, guilt, worry, fear, apathy, grief
- Cognitive: confusion, memory problems, difficulty focusing or attending to details
- Physical: sleep difficulties, exhaustion
- Behavioral: expressed anger/irritability, substance misuse, withdrawal from others, overwork, abandonment of self-care

You should anticipate family concerns about your safety and theirs.

- Complete a basic disaster preparedness kit/plan at home
- Include a family/significant other communications plan
- Identify other supports for your family (including health needs)
- For those with children, learn how to do "Listen, Protect and Connect" Psychological First Aid For Children and adult family members
  - Version for children: http://www.ready.gov/sites/default/files/documents/files/PFA_Parents.pdf
  - Version for adults: http://www.ready.gov/sites/default/files/documents/files/LPC_Booklet.pdf

You should anticipate triggers. Triggers are reminders of previous traumatic stress set off by current response via sights, sounds, smells, and thoughts.

- Event triggers can produce intense feelings seemingly "out of the blue"
- Learning to identify and anticipate event triggers can mitigate but not eliminate their impact
- Example: interacting with pediatric victims triggers images or thoughts of your own children

TIP

Remember self-care is primary, "mission critical" and not secondary.

Review of the "Anticipate" step: Anticipate your triggers in order to manage stress.

- You are building personal resilience when you begin to anticipate stressors and then think through a menu of coping responses.
- Focus of your concerns: friends, family, and self. Are they safe, am I safe?
- Traumatic and cumulative response stressors both count
- What do you think your triggers will be?

Earthquake damage and subsequent fire, Nepal 2015. Photo Courtesy of Author.

Step 2: PLAN—Create Your Anticipate, Plan, Deter Personal Coping Plan

What are your expected stress reactions following a disaster?

- In the past, what reactions have you experienced when facing stress (from relationships, finances, work, academic, etc.): sleeplessness, anxiety, anger, lack of energy, etc.?
- Please list them now

    - _____
    - _____
    - _____
    - _____
    - _____

What are your respected response challenges?

- List what you think the most stressful aspects of working on a disaster will be for you? (If you are unsure of what you might find stressful, review the lists of triggers in the Anticipate section).

   - _____
   - _____
   - _____
   - _____
   - _____

What stressors do you anticipate will be the easiest and hardest for you to deal with?

- These are your response "challenges"
- How will you react?
- What are your "resilience" factors?
- Add it all up: what's your coping plan?
- Practice your plan
   - Practice your coping skills NOW

Identify your social support system (people/organizations who can support you and who you can support during a disaster?)

- Please list them:

   - _____
   - _____
   - _____
   - _____

Plan how to reach this social support system during a disaster. This may include talking with team members, a team counselor or chaplain, or even looking a photos of your family and friends and remembering pleasant times with them. Schedule regular times to access support while on your deployment (a phone call, if available, to loved ones or an evening meal and debriefing with fellow volunteers, etc.) Prepare to provide and receive support.

Your positive coping plan.

Everyone has different ways of coping with stress. What positive methods of managing stress work best for you everyday (connecting with others vs recharging alone, exercise, meditation, prayer)? What positive techniques for managing stress do you think will work for you during and after a disaster deployment? These strategies might include taking regular breaks during your shift, a short period of exercise (5–10 minutes of calisthenics/yoga/stretching) in the mornings or evenings, listening to music as you fall asleep, relaxation breathing, visualizing an upcoming vacation or holiday, or recording or analyzing your experiences and feelings in a journal.

Using delivery truck as improvised treatment area, Port-au-Prince 2010. Photo Courtesy of Author.

TIP

It is recommended that you limit your exposure to media reports of the disaster, if those are causing you stress.

List your positive coping plan/strategies here:

- _____
- _____
- _____
- _____

Your Resilience factors.

People often find that there are positive things about working in a disaster. You should feel good about making a difference when a community needs you most. Your actions may inspire others like your family, friends and coworkers. You may be fulfilling a moral or religious obligation. Please list positive factors that might give you a sense of mission or purpose during a disaster:

- _____
- _____
- _____
- _____

Consider what might help you cope in advance.

- Build on your successful coping in everyday life
  - How do you handle typically handle stress?
- What works for you?
  - Understand the importance and the limits of your response role
  - "Prepare for the possibles, but focus on the probables"
  - Build cohesion with team members by learning their personal stories and motivation.

Review the "Plan" step: Create a coping plan in advance in order to manage stress.

- Identify your anticipated stress reactions
- Identify your anticipated response challenges
- Identify your social support system
- Identify your positive coping strategies
- Identify your resilience factors

Step 3: DETER
Activate your "Personal Resilience Plan."

- This means activating your coping plan
  - donning your mental "Personal Protective Equipment"
- Monitor your stress exposure using the PsySTART system (see below)—your stress dosimeter
  - There is are single day, "snapshot" versions, multiday personal PsySTART logs and a Team Leader record keeping form.
- Reach out for support from your social support system

- Learn what work based coping resources you have and use them if your self-triage indicates traumatic risk factors or cumulative trending of increased cumulative events.

PsySTART is a checklist based, self-triage system to help you monitor how many mental stresses you are being exposed to on a daily basis or during a multiday deployment.

"Triage" is a medical concept that emphasizes evaluating how sick or injured a patient is in order to decide who should receive treatment first when the number of affected patients overwhelms available care. The word triage comes from "trier," French for sort and the concept originated with battlefield surgeons in Napoleon's army. With limited medical resources in the heat of combat, they would rapidly evaluate wounded soldiers and decide whose injuries were minor enough that they could wait for treatment, which combatants were so badly wounded that it was a waste of resources to operate on them (they were given pain medication, if possible, and left to die) and which soldiers could be expected to survive if given immediate care. This sorting/prioritization model has spread widely throughout modern medicine and is implemented whenever the number of critical patients exceeds the capacity of available medical providers.

Using delivery truck as improvised treatment area, Port-au-Prince 2010. Photo Courtesy of Author.

"Self-triage" in this situation could be considered a bit of a misnomer, because you are always the most important patient and you should always seek treatment if you have been affected. However, triage has become synonymous with organized systems to determine severity and that is what PsySTART offers.

Single occurrence version:

PsySTART™ Disaster Mental Health Triage System

Date: 09/14/2016		Record ID: 21	
DOB: 07/16/1998 Age: 18 Years (At Time of Entry)		Sex: Male	
DID YOU WITNESS ANY SEVERE BURNS, DISMEMBERMENT, OR MUTILATIONS? (FOR EXAMPLE: CHILD WITH BURN TO MOST OF HIS/HER BODY SURFACE)			
WERE YOU EXPOSED TO PATIENTS WITH PROLONGED SCREAMING DUE TO PAIN OR FEAR?			
DID YOU WITNESS ANY PATIENT DEATH OR OTHER SEVERE INJURIES? (FOR EXAMPLE: AMPUTATION, EVISCERATION, OR DEATH OF PATIENTS WHO WERE UNDER YOUR CARE OR UNDER THE CARE OF YOUR TEAM)			
WERE YOU ASKED TO PERFORM DUTIES OUTSIDE OF YOUR CURRENT SKILLS? (FOR EXAMPLE: TREATING ADULTS ALTHOUGH YOU ARE A PEDIATRICIAN OR DOING A MAJOR SURGICAL PROCEDURE ALTHOUGH YOU ARE NOT A SURGEON)			
DID YOU EXPERIENCED ANY HAZARDOUS WORKING CONDITIONS? (FOR EXAMPLE: EXTREME SHIFT LENGTH, COMPROMISED SITE SAFETY/SECURITY, OR OTHER ISSUES)			
DID ANY SERIOUS INJURY, ILLNESS, OR DEATH OCCURS AMONG YOUR COWORKERS?			
WERE YOU UNABLE TO COMMUNICATE REGULARLY WITH YOUR OWN FAMILY OR SIGNIFICANT OTHERS?			
DID YOU FEEL YOUR LIFE WAS IN DANGER?			
WERE YOU FORCED TO ABANDON A PATIENT? (FOR EXAMPLE: LEAVING A LIVING PATIENT BECAUSE OF UNSAFE SITUATION OR OTHER FACTORS)			
WERE YOU DIRECTLY IMPACTED BY THE INCIDENT AT WORK OR AT HOME?			
WERE YOU RESPONSIBLE FOR MAKING EXPECTANT TRIAGE (TRIAGE AS BLACK AND LEFT TO DIE) DECISIONS? (FOR EXAMPLE: DETERMINING THAT UNDER EXISTING CARE/SURGE CIRCUMSTANCES THAT NO EMERGENT CARE WAS OFFERED)			
WERE YOU UNABLE TO MEET YOUR PATIENT€™S CRITICAL NEEDS AT TIMES? (FOR EXAMPLE: LACK OF RESOURCES SUCH AS A DRUGS, LABORATORY, IMAGING, PATIENT SURGE, OR CRISIS STANDARD OF CARE CONDITIONS)			
DID YOU HAVE DIRECT CONTACT WITH MANY GRIEVING FAMILY MEMBERS?			
DID YOU HAVE CONCERNS ABOUT THE SAFETY OR WELL-BEING OF YOUR OWN FAMILY MEMBERS, SIGNIFICANT OTHERS, OR PETS WHILE YOU WERE DEPLOYED?			
DID YOU EXPERIENCE ANY SERIOUS INJURY OR ILLNESSES AS A RESULT OF YOUR DEPLOYMENT ?			
DID YOU WITNESS PEDIATRIC DEATHS OR SEVERE INJURIES?			
DID YOU WITNESS AN UNUSUALLY HIGH NUMBER OF DEATHS?			
UNABLE TO RETURN HOME?			
DO(DID) YOU HAVE HEALTH CONCERNS FOR SELF DUE TO POSSIBLE AGENT/TOXIC EXPOSURE(BIOLOGICAL,CHEMICAL, RADIOLOGICAL/NUCLEAR)?			
I AM NOT RECEIVING SUFFICIENT SUPPORT FROM OTHERS			
NO TRIAGE FACTORS			✓

2002-2016 M.Schreiber

Confidential Information

PsySTART Staff Self-Triage System Instructions

Complete any identifying information on the top, including the reporting period, your job and department. The form is voluntary and your name is optional.

At the end of your shift each day:

- *Check the box for each experience that has occurred.* If you have other concerns, feel free to write them in the space provided in Question #19.
- *Review stress management strategies and your own personal coping strategies.* Even if you only checked one experience or you checked several items, it is important to monitor your stress early and continue doing so throughout the incident response.
- *Share your responses.* If you feel comfortable, consider sharing your responses with mental health, spiritual care, social services or other staff providing assistance for further coping ideas, support, and assistance.
- *If you answered Yes to #17,* please follow up with the appropriate staff in charge or your personal mental health provider during the incident or as soon as possible.

At the end of your incident response:

- *Review your totals.* Tally your responses for each day and write them down in the daily total box.
- *Share your responses.* For any checked items or other concerns, consider sharing your self-observation information with mental/spiritual health personnel or other appropriate staff in charge of employee wellbeing during the incident. Remember to monitor your stress during the response and activate your coping plan early. You can revise your coping plan accordingly to maximize your resilience. Review your plan 30 days postincident, if not sooner.

The PsySTART Staff Self-Triage System was developed to help personnel assess themselves following a disaster. This system can help you take steps to implement personal coping strategies or seek follow-up with mental health/spiritual care or other resources. Completing this form can also help your organization determine areas of need for staff and offer resources for prioritization.

This self-triage system measures potentially stressful experiences during an incident. It does not measure overall mental health status or mental health symptoms and it does not provide any mental health diagnosis. This tool helps you monitor certain stressful experiences that may occur in incidents that are associated with risk for extended distress and/or stress symptoms. Checking a box only indicates that you've experienced the item that day, but you can use this tool to monitor experiences across multiple days of an incident. The total number of checked items may indicate a cumulative "dose" of stressful experiences and you can use this information to facilitate your own stress management strategies. You can also share your responses with your organization's employee health, mental health, spiritual care or social services staff member or another team member for more coping ideas.

As you can see, the system is designed to evaluate the stresses and triggers responders are experiencing as they serve the needs of victims of the disaster. These stresses and triggers are associated with their volunteer duties. However, it is possible that you or other members of your team could be directly affected by the disaster (becoming victims yourselves). There could be an aftershock, a secondary storm or fire or something else which moves you from the responder category into one the people suffering the affects of the incident. If outside of your work setting you also had other stressors, you would use the PsyStart for Victims form. You can see it deals with the direct impacts of the disaster, rather than the secondary consequences of responding to it.

PsySTART™ Disaster Mental Health Triage System

LAST NAME	FIRST NAME	MEDICAL RECORD NUMBER
AGE	GENDER	HOME ZIP CODE
	MALE FEMALE	

INDICATE "YES"
ANSWERS BELOW

	MARKING EXAMPLES
EXPRESSED THOUGHT OR INTENT TO HARM SELF/OTHERS?	
FELT OR EXPRESSED EXTREME PANIC?	CORRECT
FELT DIRECT THREAT TO LIFE OF SELF OR FAMILY MEMBER?	
SAW / HEARD DEATH OR SERIOUS INJURY OF OTHER?	
MULTIPLE DEATHS OF FAMILY, FRIENDS OR PEERS?	WRONG
DEATH OF IMMEDIATE FAMILY MEMBER?	
DEATH OF FRIEND OR PEER?	WRONG
DEATH OF PET?	
SIGNIFICANT DISASTER RELATED ILLNESS OR PHYSICAL INJURY OF SELF OR FAMILY MEMBER?	
TRAPPED OR DELAYED EVACUATION?	
HOME NOT LIVABLE DUE TO DISASTER?	
FAMILY MEMBER CURRENTLY MISSING OR UNACCOUNTED FOR?	
CHILD CURRENTLY SEPARATED FROM ALL CARETAKERS?	
FAMILY MEMBERS SEPARATED AND UNAWARE OF THEIR LOCATION/STATUS DURING DISASTER?	
PRIOR HISTORY OF MENTAL HEALTH CARE?	
CONFIRMED EXPOSURE/CONTAMINATION TO AGENT?	
DE-CONTAMINATED?	
RECEIVED MEDICAL TREATMENT FOR EXPOSURE/CONTAMINATION?	
HEALTH CONCERNS TIED TO EXPOSURE?	
NO TRIAGE FACTORS IDENTIFIED?	

EMERGENCY MEDICAL
SERVICES AGENCY

Original – Patient Chart   Funded through HHS HPP grant #6 U3REP060070
For use with the PsySTART Incident Management System

If the situation escalates and you are no longer a responder but have become a patient or victim, be honest with yourself. It is probably best for you to stop your efforts to assist and return home to seek treatment (psychological or medical) as soon as possible. If you try to continue volunteering in the disaster zone while attempting to get help for your needs, you are most likely an ineffective worker and also taking valuable resources away from local victims.

In addition to the Individual version of PsyStart, there is an online Leader version available in some areas. It is a log in which the person monitoring the mental health of your team can track how many members on each day experienced each trigger. The goal would be for this record to be used proactively to identify trends and solve problems for your group and for others that come after you. If team members are expressing concern over performing duties outside their current skills, or that they are experiencing hazardous working conditions, leadership should be addressing these issues if possible as they occur rather than letting them continue.

PsySTART Staff Self-Triage System

Team Leader Summary Form Instructions
At the end of each reporting period (shift/day):

- *Determine method for gathering employee self-triage information:* collecting individual PsySTART forms, group debriefing, one-on-one interviews, etc.
- *Fill in staff totals.* For each day, write the total number of responses in the box responses received for each experience.
- *Tally affirmative responses.* For each day, write the total number of responses in the box at the bottom of that day's column.
- *Tally number of team members.* For each day, write the total number of team members that responded in the box at the bottom of that day's column.
- *Tally number of risk factors.* For each risk factor, write in the number of affirmative answers for that risk factor during the incident in the box at the end of the row.
- *Review information to determine individual and collective risk/stress patterns.* Refer to Health and Well-Being Job Action Sheet (see below) to:
  - Provide assistance for individual team members who may desire further assistance.
  - Identify common risk/stress trends affecting all team members for next steps to mitigate risk/stress.

The PsySTART Staff Self-Triage System was developed to help responders assess themselves following a disaster. The Team Leader Summary Form provides awareness for Health and Well-Being unit leaders on the total level of risk exposure for members of their team and an estimate of the aggregated risk experience for the entire team. This information can help leaders proactively respond to the acute needs of individuals and also at the overall team level.

Health and Well-Being Unit Leader

In Chapter 3, Developing Relevant Training and Education for Deployments, we discussed the Incident Command System (ICS). As an example, you will see below, in a large hospital incident command structure (HICS), under the Logistics Section, there is a Support Branch, and under that there is a Health and Well-being Unit Leader.

Hospital Incident Management Team

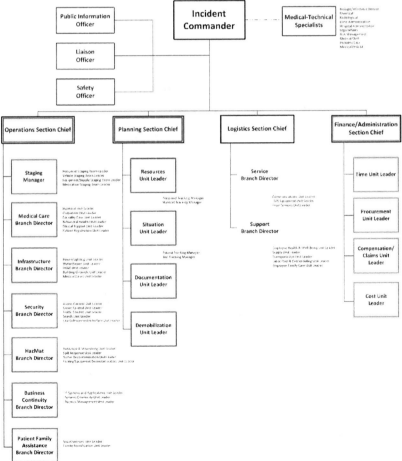

There are dozens of positions listed in this organizational chart and it is unlikely that smaller teams would staff most or all of them and probably wouldn't have an entire unit dedicated to health and well-being. However, responder mental and physical health are critical and at least one of your team members should have the training, experience and commitment to monitor them. The team leader, assistant team leader, behavioral health specialist or chaplain may have that task in addition to other duties.

Like every position in ICS, there is a Task Sheet for the Health and Well-being Unit Leader. The task sheet serves as a reminder of important concerns for that position. Feel free to modify one to add their PsySTART responsibilities. If you want these task sheets and other documentation for HICS, they are available for free through the California Emergency Medical Services Authority website.

CONCLUSION

Please use the tools in this chapter in a "building block" approach to increasing your readiness to respond. If you are able to find local volunteer opportunities, or a scheduled/nonemergency overseas deployment, fill out the PsySTART checklist for these experiences. You may feel foolish doing so if you record no stressors or triggers, or you may be surprised that these "routine" activities are more stressful than you anticipated. Either way you are practicing Dr. Schreiber's valuable system, which will help you and your team in your actual disaster deployment.

As noted in previous chapters, good physical condition and having the appropriate equipment and training are critical to your success as a disaster volunteer. However, nothing is more important than constructing and maintaining your psychological resilience in the face of the stressors you will encounter. If your equipment fails or you become sick or injured but you are able to maintain your psychological resilience, your overall volunteer experience will probably still be positive.

Disaster Case Study: 2004 Indian Ocean Tsunami

At approximately 8 am Indonesian local time on December 26, 2004 a 9.1 magnitude earthquake off the coast of Sumatra caused a number of tsunamis (oversized ocean waves triggered by seismic activity or undersea events) to strike the coasts of neighboring countries. The tsunamis caused approximately 230,000 deaths, hundreds of thousands of injuries and extreme environmental and economic damage. Indonesia, the Aceh province in particular, suffered the most casualties, but Sri Lanka, India, and Thailand were also heavily impacted.

The word "tsunami" is from Japanese, meaning "harbor wave" and stems from past tragedies when Japanese fishermen would return from an uneventful day on the ocean and find their port communities devastated by these mysterious events. In the open ocean, tsunamis move at incredible speeds (often over 500 mph/800 kmph), and may be 100+ miles (160+ km) in width but are virtually unnoticeable as 12 in. (0.3 m) high swells. When they reach coastal areas they slow down to 50 mph (80 kmph) or less and their height increases drastically as energy is transferred from velocity and width to elevation. In 1958, a landslide in Lituya Bay, Alaska initiated the largest tsunami on record: 1700 ft (524 m) high.

When they struck the shore, waves from the Indian Ocean tsunami have been documented at 100 ft (30 m) high and were especially overwhelming due to the low elevation of many of the affected areas. From local reports, the first tsunami struck Banda Aceh, an Indonesian city of 220,000, within 20 minutes of the earthquake, with a second, larger wave following 15–20 minutes later. The city's highest naturally occurring land only has an elevation of 33 ft (10 m) so the tsunamis swept inland almost 2.5 miles (4 km) and were catastrophic, killing over 160,000 residents.

Responding organizations theorize that women and children were disproportionately affected, as they may have been waiting on or near beaches for fishermen in their families to return with the morning's catch. Economic capacities such as fishing, tourism, and farming palm and coconut products were also damaged for years to come. Thousands of foreign tourists were also vacationing in these beach areas during the Christmas holidays and while they may have had more financial resources than poorer residents, they also struggled with local language and geographical awareness as the disaster struck.

Other complicating factors included longstanding insurgent conflicts in two of the most impacted areas: the Free Aceh (Gam) movement in Indonesia and the Tamil Tigers in Sri Lanka. Both groups immediately declared cease-fires to assist victims of the disaster but there were squabbles over armed forces entering rebel territory to help residents and who would be able to receive and administer the massive amounts of foreign aid flowing to the regions. Despite high levels of distrust between the national governments and the two groups of independence fighters, there were no reports of aid workers being targeted. However, that potential was a serious concern for disaster responders.

After the tsunami, the Gam movement and the Indonesian government were able to use the disaster rebuilding process to create a peaceful political solution to their conflict. The area was granted increased autonomy in return for remaining a part of Indonesia and rebel fighters laid down their arms. In contrast, after an initial ceasefire, the Tamil Tigers and the Sri Lankan government resumed hostilities and approximately 40,000 more died in the fighting before the region was forcefully pacified by government troops by 2009. These alternative endings show the positive and negative possibilities as communities recover from a disaster.

While no foreign disaster responders were targeted after this tsunami, ask yourself whether that would be true in areas controlled by organizations such as Islamic State in Levant (ISIL) and Al Qaeda? There have been numerous accounts of journalists and aid workers captured, tortured and killed during ongoing relief efforts in their territories. Would you be willing to respond to a disaster facing those risks? What information would you try to gather before traveling to a disaster area in the midst of an armed conflict? What local connections/intelligence does your volunteer group have there?

Consider the same questions we have asked in the other case studies: travel—major unaffected airports in the region, local weather/conditions, appropriate equipment/shelter/supplies, victim needs/fears? Now use Dr. Schreiber's Anticipate, Plan, Deter lessons from this chapter—make a practice list of your concerns, potential stressors, resources, and strengths for the Indian Ocean Tsunami.

CHAPTER 7

On Deployment I: Setup, Operations, and Self-Care

You have not lived today until you have done something for someone who can never repay you.

John Bunyan

THE CALL ... AND THE TACTICAL PAUSE

You've gotten the call. You have been activated. Perhaps it's a planned volunteer trip or an actual disaster deployment. You have been preparing for this for months. You have your lists, your equipment, your supplies, and your certifications ready. However, especially if it is a disaster mission, you will be rushing around for the next 24–48 hours, buying last minute items, printing out documents, and one hundred other tasks.

Stop.

There is a concept in military operations called the "tactical pause." In essence, this means that in the period immediately preceding (if possible) or following a life-critical event, you take a few minutes to figure out your priorities and next steps rather than reacting instinctively and possibly poorly.

A real-life example is that you may be in a disaster zone and an aftershock causes a building to collapse in front of you. You want to immediately rush in and pull debris away, searching for survivors. That's a natural human instinct. However, evaluate the situation before you do so. Remember Management by Objectives from the

Incident Command System overview? Take a moment or two to figure out your goals and your challenges.

Building collapse, Nepal 2015. Photo Courtesy of Author.

Are there looming hazards like parts of the building still standing precariously, which without reinforcement, could fall on you or other rescuers? (A rule of thumb is that debris from a collapsing structure can reach one and a half times its own height. So, if you have a damaged 20-ft (7 m) high building, chimney or column in front of you, you don't want to lay victims down or set up operations less than 30 ft (10 m) away. And, in general, corners of buildings are stronger than long, unsupported stretches of wall.)

Do you smell gas or see other hazardous conditions? Have you confirmed that nearby wires are no longer carrying electrical current? Have you called back to your organization, told them you were okay, your location and that you needed help with this new situation? Have you attempted to create or join an improvised or official management structure so that someone is aware of all the activities going on in the disaster scene, and one set of responders is not digging into part of the building which will cause a collapse on other responders? Becoming a victim will obviously hurt you and your team, but it will also probably mean that efforts to reach the original victims will be delayed or halted. The truth is that saving the lives of international responders would most likely take priority over helping locals.

That's a dramatic example but stopping an instant to plan, in the time before you depart for a deployment, is just as important. Take a tactical pause every few hours. Review your packing, medical, document, communications, and travel checklists. Create lists of your checklists, if needed. Have you completed the PsySTART forms or will you have time to do so on the plane? Realize that there are "nice-to-have" and "need-to-have" items on your shopping and to-do lists. Prioritize these categories. Delegate some errands to friends and family. They will probably be excited and proud to help support your endeavors to respond to this disaster dominating the headlines.

Keep the concept of the tactical pause in the back of your mind during the deployment. As your team arrives in the area, you may be confronted by a collapsed building, a crowd of injured or hungry victims, or another urgent situation. It seems counterintuitive to take a few minutes to bring your group together for a very quick planning session about how you will divide the building to search it, or how you will set up your treatment or supply distribution area. And, it might be best, if possible, to have this meeting out of view of those affected who wouldn't understand why you are not helping immediately. However, you may save time and lives by having a plan rather than rushing in without one.

TEAM BUILDING

Ideally, you would have been working with your volunteer team for months before the disaster strikes. You would be familiar with them and they with you. However, especially at the beginning of your volunteer experiences, you may be finding opportunities with short notice or your organization might be pulling group members from across the country(ies) who have never met before.

Because of this, you may be meeting your crew for the first time at the airport in your home city, or in a terminal thousands of miles away. Try to get to know each of them as you wait for the next leg of travel, or in advance if possible. Your organization should have issued you a roster of team member names, positions, phone numbers, and email addresses. Check each person off as you connect a face with a name.

There is a description of team dynamics called Tuckman's Model. It states that there are five distinct stages of group evolution:

1. Forming—The members initiate efforts to build trust and establish an identity and agree on goals.
2. Storming—Personalities and other individual characteristics cause conflict within the group.
3. Norming—The group is able to resolve the clashes and becomes closer.
4. Performing—Everyone is working well together to accomplish the objective(s).
5. Mourning/adjourning—The group disbands and individuals may suffer from grief over its loss.

I have found every one of these stages has occurred on all my deployments.

Hopefully your group leader will facilitate some icebreakers in which you can find out backgrounds, motivations, specialties, and strengths. If not, take some time to chat with each of your team. A simple but effective icebreaker is to put a number of coins into a hat and have group members draw them out and then say where they were/what they were doing the year the coin was minted (you may optimize the results by ensuring all the coins are from the past 10 to 20 years). Icebreakers force quiet participants to introduce themselves but give also everyone a chance to establish the identity they want to project: witty, profound, caring, etc.

Along those lines, studies have shown that groups coalesce more quickly if members describe something meaningful about themselves in their initial interactions and show some vulnerability. This is not an invitation to over-share the intimate details of your life as an introduction, but consider the icebreaker an opportunity to be honest and interesting and not just a formality to rush through.

You will find disaster response attracts a wide range of tempera-ments from quietly devote to loudly religious, atheists, agnostics, from risk-takers and big-talkers to humble hard workers. Your personality may be introverted or extroverted, but I urge you to come out of your shell if you are quiet or give others a chance to tell their stories if you know you tend to dominate conversations.

TIP

Wear badges or pieces of tape with your names on them, at least for the first few days. This is especially helpful for your local partners, for whom your foreign names might be exotic, hard to remember, and hard to pronounce.

Outdoor clinic with tarps for shade, Nepal 2015. Photo Courtesy of Author.

Sleep on the plane if you can, but otherwise I offer that this is not the time to bury yourself in a book, the in-flight movies, or isolated in your headphones. Get to know your team. If you are not sitting near someone, find them in the aisle or near the bathrooms. Even a few minutes of conversation and familiarity will pay dividends in your team building. Once you hit the disaster area, your opportunities to do so in a nonstressed situation will be very limited.

Conversely, the bulk of your group may be traveling together, with a few stragglers meeting you at the final destination or flying in a day or two earlier or later. I have been that lone addition and it was daunting to see that the team had already bonded before I met them and knew each other's nicknames, food preferences, and pet jokes. Make sure these late arrivals are welcomed in. There will be people you connect with more readily because of your personalities, histories, and senses of humor but avoid cliques and hanging out with only a select few. The goal of the mission is not to have the best conversations with people most compatible with you, but to make the strongest team, and that means bringing everyone into the interaction.

Advance Team

As we discussed, you will (ideally) not be the team leader/organizer on your first overseas deployment, but the advance team concept is one you should be familiar with.

When an organization considers whether to send a group of volunteers to assist in a disaster, there are a number of questions which need to be answered. Some of the broader issues like what services are needed may be answered by media reports and appeals for assistance from the local government or the United Nations.

The more specific concerns such as overall safety and security, how will volunteers travel to the affected area, where will they stay, how will they get food, water and resupply themselves, where will they work, local partners, translators, etc., will most likely need to be answered by an in-person reconnaissance of the situation. Many volunteer organizations choose to send a two to four person advance team to evaluate the disaster before a full 10–30 member group arrives. Each advance team volunteer may have a specialty to focus on, such as medical treatment areas, setting up housing for incident victims, communications, water supply, or financial recovery.

I strongly advocate the advance team model because I believe it saves a lot of time. By the nature of a calamity, typical societal structures have broken down. This ensures that finding transportation, housing, food, water, and local partners take much longer than normal. You will try to meet a key local contact but discover they are out getting supplies and won't return for hours. Mobile phones are working poorly, if at all, so many conversations must happen in person. One or more of the advance team members will have to simply wait for critical consultations or information. However, I think it is far more efficient for two to four of the advance members to "waste" these hours than for the entire team to kill time while these arrangements are being made.

The advance team will probably divide responsibilities such as finding food and water, lodging, etc. But, it remains a team, responsible for each other. The concept becomes much riskier when an individual is sent to work alone in the disaster area. That is not a generally accepted practice.

Lastly, from the moments the disaster is first reported, effective volunteer organizations are leveraging their relationships abroad to find needed resources (information, local contacts, and supplies) in the affected areas. They may be reaching out to religious denominations in the region, service groups like the Lions Club and Rotary International, or professional groups such as medical, engineering, or technical associations. They may even be posting on social media to find people in your country who can connect them with friends or family members who could provide local assistance once the team arrives. I cannot overemphasize how important these connections are. While everything these residents say should be evaluated carefully, like any other source of information, the locals will know who needs help, who has space, where to get supplies, etc.

Author with Filipino surgeons, Tacloban 2013. Photo Courtesy of Author.

Also, be prepared for prospective contacts to fall through as you work in postdisaster chaos. When I deployed to the 2012 typhoon in the Philippines with Hope Force International (HFI), I was on our advance team. As a primary deployment plan, HFI used long-standing connections with another large and established disaster response group. Their leadership in Europe assured us that their advance team, already in the Philippines, would share vehicles and hotel rooms with us and that we could combine medical operations. Unfortunately, that message had not reached their personnel on the ground. When we arrived at their hotel on the outskirts of the disaster zone, the other group was not expecting us. They were facing a transportation shortage and were wary about accepting medical professionals who had not been vetted by their human resources department. That night we were able to stay in their hotel room, which was welcome, but the next day each group set off on their own. No hard feelings, that's what working in a disaster zone is like.

Our backup contact was a local businessman in the city of Tacloban. He turned out to be a fantastic resource as he set up meetings with a local hospital administrator, partnered us with a visiting Filipino surgical team, and arranged for our lodgings in empty several apartments he and his colleagues owned.

> **TIP**
>
> Whether you are on the advance team or the full group, you will probably find there are unused hours or even days, as you set up to address areas of need. Patience and flexibility are key to working in a disaster zone. Sort your equipment, organize your supplies, fill the time productively. You are eager to help, not sit around, but try not to get frustrated by these delays.

HOUSING, UNPACKING, ESCAPE ROUTE, AND RALLY PLAN

Once you've arrived in the disaster area, you should going to your lodging or staging area. You will be putting the lessons of your hiking or camping expeditions to use. If you are staying in a tent, find a location away from overhead hazards, noisy generators, and heavily trafficked areas if possible. Where will you get water? Where are the facilities in which you can relieve/wash yourself? You may be staying inside a building. Was it damaged in the incident? Has a licensed engineer evaluated it and determined that it is safe for habitation? Is there running water and/or electricity? Have you brought a carbon monoxide detector if you are sleeping or working near generators?

Seismic damage to walls in guest house, Nepal 2015. Photo Courtesy of Author.

You picked your luggage because you could operate out of it effectively without a chest of drawers or other furniture. Organize your clothing, equipment, and supplies. Hang your mosquito net, if needed. Make sure you have your headlamp or other light source nearby in case of a middle of the night emergency. Do you have an escape route planned out in case of an aftershock, a fire, or another event? Has your team established a meeting point where the group will assemble to make sure everyone has gotten out safely?

If you have free time, does your organization have a policy on whether you can go out into the disaster zone and look around? If that exploration is allowed, it's best to bring a local contact, tell your team leadership when you will return, and bring a buddy from your group. Though you have a local guide, practice staying oriented so you could return without their help. For even a short walkabout, bring a daypack with food, water, a flashlight, first aid supplies, and ideally a communications device. Remember, you have no idea what you will encounter out there.

What's the security situation? Do you need an escort when you walk the streets? During the 2014 Typhoon Haiyan in the Philippines, local jailers set several hundred inmates free as flood waters rose. After the storm, this led to major fears of crime from the populace. Can you leave bags open and unlocked during the day or do you need to secure them every morning? Are you planning to leave an expensive solar charger out all day on a windowsill or ledge? What do your local contacts recommend? Are you carrying your own currency, which will need to be changed or local money, if there are supplies or food to purchase?

Debris field, Leyte, Philippines 2013. Photo Courtesy of Mike Morse Photography.

Communications

How will you communicate during the disaster? Are there satellite phones or portable radios being distributed? Do you have the radio channels, and relevant parties at home have those phone numbers? Does everyone have a common communications capability or application like WhatsApp or Facebook? It is highly unlikely all of you will have satellite phones, but each of you should have the numbers for every phone on the deployment and for multiple key contacts in your home country, and everyone on the team should know how to operate the satellite phones in case of emergency. The small, camping-style portable walky-talkies seem like a good idea, but I have found that when they are operated in an urban area with many buildings their range is severally limited, often to a city block or less. Also, they use a lot of disposable batteries and/or their rechargeable batteries need frequent support.

Often the communications plan is to buy several inexpensive local mobile phones as soon as you arrive (depending on the disaster, cellular systems are usually functioning again within 3–5 days), or to buy local SIM cards and insert them into your personal phones. I have never seen this work as smoothly as we had hoped. It can be difficult to buy the phones, and the SIM cards, and the minutes/data for the cards, and get them all working operating in a foreign language on an unfamiliar system. We have always needed a local to guide us through the process. Then we all have to share the new phone numbers and make sure we are dialing the correct city and country codes. It's doable-just don't assume it will be easy.

In Chapter 8, On Deployment II: Continued Operations, Winding Down, and Getting Back to the "Real World," we will discuss ongoing disaster operations, further self-care, wrapping up and heading home.

Organization Profile

Tzu Chi Foundation

The Tzu Chi Foundation is a relief organization, based on Buddhist teachings, created in Taiwan in 1966. It focuses on charity, medicine, education, and humanity. In addition, Tzu Chi volunteers work in international disaster assistance, protecting the environment, bone marrow donation, and encouraging volunteerism. The foundation has been accepted by the United Nations Economic and Social Council as an official consultant and has over 10 million members in 45 countries. Volunteers do not need to be Buddhist to work with Tzu Chi.

Cheng Yen is the Taiwanese Buddhist nun who founded Tzu Chi. During her childhood, several family members died from illnesses and her community suffered under Japanese authorities during World War II. These experiences drew her into a life of service, with particular compassion to grieving and victimized populations. Three years after being initiated as a nun, Cheng Yen had a conversation with three visiting Roman Catholic sisters. They pointed out that the Catholic Church had established a network of schools and medical facilities to aid the poor, while the Buddhist faith had focused on individual conversions. That contrast, as well as her exposure to local medical procedures limited to those who could pay in advance, motivated her to initiate a modest charity effort. Thirty original participants placed a few cents each day into bamboo savings banks and the group was able to assist 15 families the first year alone.

From these humble methods, the outreach grew dramatically. Eight years after it was founded, the Tzu Chi Foundation opened its first free clinic. In 1986 it opened its first hospital and 3 years later a nursing school. In 1992 recognizing an unmet need, the foundation began registering bone marrow donors. They have gone on to found a medical school, a university and to encourage organ and cadaver donation, and recycling efforts. Due to longstanding political differences between Taiwan and the mainland, Tzu Chi was eager to assist after the 1991 floods in Central China. They were able to do so by following a strict policy of avoiding political, commercial, or religious discussions during disaster deployments, which continues to this day.

In the past two decades, Tzu Chi volunteers have responded to nearly every major global disaster, including the 9/11 terror attacks, the Indian Ocean tsunamis, Super Typhoon Haiyan, and Hurricane Sandy. Their volunteers hand out blankets made from recycled materials; distribute preloaded credit cards and vegetarian meals to victims, staff medical teams; and organize debris removal and other areas of disaster response.

Like other large charities, at times Tzu Chi has faced criticism for its staff compensation, projects, and fund-raising. If you are interested in volunteering with them, do a diligent search on their history, mission, and practices. Meet with them in person and see if you would be a good fit.

Case Study:

Haiti Earthquake 2012

A 7.0 magnitude earthquake struck Port-au-Prince, the capital of the Caribbean island nation of Haiti, at 4:53 pm local time on Tuesday, January 12, 2012. Estimates of the death toll ranged from 100,000 to 200,000, with hundreds of thousands more injured by collapsing buildings and millions left homeless.

Haiti is an impoverished country, heavily dependent on foreign assistance for healthcare, construction, food and financial aid even before the earthquake. Due to poverty, many developing countries like Haiti do not enforce building codes or have an organized emergency response system, making them especially vulnerable to disasters. Most of the concrete blocks used for construction are handmade from sand and gravel on the side of the road, with no strength standards or testing. The blocks fell to pieces during the shaking. Strong aftershocks rocked the region for weeks after the quake, creating new injuries and damage and leading many residents to sleep outside, rather than returning to their homes, intact or not.

Port-au-Prince is a teeming city with numerous unreinforced concrete multistory structures holding millions of residents, workers, and students. The earthquake destroyed thousands of these buildings, trapping, killing, and injuring hundreds of thousands of victims. Additionally, government buildings, hospitals, utility providers, roads, the international airport, and the port were all severely damaged.

Haiti faced endemic problems such as corruption, violent crime, malaria and other tropical diseases, lack of access to healthcare, education, affordable food, housing and clean water which had occurred for decades before this disaster. Furthermore, competing Haitian government regimes had seized, reseized, or nationalized hundreds of private properties over the years (giving them to their supporters). When it came time for international aid organizations to help residents rebuild, there were often multiple claims for every acre of land.

Questions to consider:

- How would the time of day of the disaster or the amount of warning affect the local population in a disaster?
- Which methods of communications may or may not still be working?
- How do you expect an aid organization would transport you to such a damaged area?
- What types of injuries, illness, or mental trauma do you predict you might see?
- What precautions would you want to take to protect yourself?
- If your charitable organization begins to offer a commodity such as food, medical care, or clothing for free after a disaster, what happens to locals who previously depended on selling these things to survive?
  - What types of long-term recovery issues would a community like this face? Reconstruction, debris management from collapsed buildings and ruined belongings, abandoned pets, rebuilding communications, and other infrastructures?

CHAPTER 8

On Deployment II: Continued Operations, Winding Down, and Getting Back to the "Real World"

Character cannot be developed in ease and quiet. Only through experience of trial and suffering can the soul be strengthened, ambition inspired, and success achieved.

Helen Keller

In a book on disaster volunteering, are you surprised that only two chapters out of nine cover the actual deployment? Once you are on the ground, you will be thrown into a unique situation and will be busy fulfilling the responsibilities your group has assigned you. No one can describe in advance the conditions you will be working in and there will be few opportunities for additional training, finding new equipment, or experimenting with team dynamics. Hopefully you have seen how critical the months and years of preparation leading up to the disaster are.

Having said that, here are a few more recommendations for the remainder of your deployment.

TRANSPORTATION AND RECORDKEEPING

Especially in poorer countries, traffic accidents are a major source of fatalities and serious injuries. Mopeds, motorcycles, and mototaxis are popular and practical, but riders are especially exposed on crowded, poorly maintained, and chaotic roads. For this reason, some relief organizations have prohibited their staff from using these lightweight vehicles. Your group, and you personally, will have to make a determination on their use. I have found a major safety issue is that there are never any extra helmets when you are using a motorcycle or moped in a disaster zone. A risky situation becomes much more dangerous when even a low-speed fall off the back of a bike could be tragic. I have added a lightweight hockey-style plastic helmet to my basic equipment to provide some minimum protection, despite the odd looks I might get wearing it on the back of a moto.

Moto taxi, Nepal 2015. Photo Courtesy of Author.

As I recommended at the beginning of this book, you should be keeping a journal. I think this is especially important on your actual deployment. Even if you use 5 minutes in the morning or evening and these are just stream of consciousness impressions you type into the notes section of your smart phone, the process is valuable. If you plan on having future disaster volunteering experiences, you should be keeping a list of what is working, what isn't, and what you should have brought with you. Everytime I deploy, I come back with new ideas. And, you may think that you can recollect these lessons without writing them down, but the lack of sleep, long hours, and sensory overload will probably defeat your memory.

Most likely, you will also be taking pictures. That's fine, but investigate the policies of your organization, especially in regard to posting on social media. Be sensitive to the tragedies you are documenting. The ruined building you are photographing may still hold the bodies of someone's family. If you wouldn't shoot a picture of a medical patient without their permission in your home country, why would you assume it's okay to do so in a foreign disaster zone?

By using a journal or photography, you are remembering the important moments: good or bad, inspiring, funny or sad. This is also a mental health self-care tool. You are beginning to process these experiences as you document them. Finally, your materials may become the basis for something you create after the deployment. You could be asked to make a presentation on your volunteer work to your school, job, place of worship, or club. It may be important to you to raise money for victims of the disaster once you return home, and these resources can help your efforts. After one of my disaster responses, I wrote an article for a professional journal and I relied heavily on the notes and statistics I had gathered during the deployment. It felt good that other responders could learn from my account.

We will talk more about the postdisaster phase of your experiences in the last chapters, but talking, writing or exhibiting photos/videos are all ways you can later use to find meaning in the devastation you witnessed. Just make sure that, unless you are the team photographer, your primary focus on the deployment is getting your job done, not compiling the ultimate selfie highlight reel.

It is also a responsible practice to keep official statistics and records of the aid you are giving. A major complaint about foreign teams is that they give short-term assistance with no long-term follow through. I have experienced this as locals requested care from our group and stated that they had been seen several days earlier by another international organization. The patients had been given a verbal explanation and a bag of pills by the previous caregiver, but no written diagnosis or instructions. Often we couldn't even figure out what medications the patient had been taking or whether those had been helping. Likewise, bring your statistics to the coordination meetings your group should be participating in with local and international responders. These authorities need situational awareness of how many wells are being dug, houses being rebuilt, patients being treated for various conditions, etc. In particular, the medical trend data can help them identify disease outbreaks in their early stages, rather than after they have spread. The local emergency managers need to know which areas have been searched, have received aid, are being overlooked, etc.

Public health disease tracking by hand, Tacloban 2013. Photo Courtesy of Author.

We discussed the United Nations (UN) Cluster system in Chapter 2, Finding and Choosing the Right Volunteer Organization. Their coordination meetings can be perceived as tedious, bureaucratic, and taking time away from your "real work" of helping the victims. Those criticisms may be valid at times, but the meetings still play an important role in sharing information from the field level up, and from the national and local government level down. You will be a professional responder so there is no excuse for your organization not to send at least one representative to register upon arrival and then do follow-up progress reports every few days. If you are unsure where the meetings are being held, ask the other foreign aid groups in your specialty. Their members probably will be easy to identify as other outsiders wearing medical scrubs, jumpsuits and helmets, or khaki vests.

As they have never been in a disaster before, many victims and local responders will have no idea about the Cluster system. They will be operating without the information and resources presented at these meetings. In the Philippines, the National Health Service offered local hospitals in the disaster zone a stipend for every patient seen by a foreign medical team on their property. I learned about this financial opportunity at a Health Cluster meeting and passed this on to the facility administrator who was hosting our volunteer group. The administrator was ecstatic. Likewise, at another meeting, the World Health Organization (WHO) offered free polio vaccines to any aid group that agreed to administer them to locals, and return records of their immunization operations. As the need for our clinical services declined after a week or two, we partnered with local nurses and military transport to give polio vaccinations in several rural villages. This ensured we weren't sitting around the last few days of our deployment.

Evacuation center census tracking by hand, Tacloban 2013. Photo Courtesy of Author.

SELF-CARE

Over the past few chapters we have discussed the importance of mental and physical health.

Psychological

Use the PsySTART system ... every day. Add your own coping mechanisms of a few minutes of calisthenics in the mornings or evenings or some meditation to ease the stress you are experiencing. Write in your journal. Come together after each shift with your teammates and discuss the good, the bad, and the ugly.

Your body may hold on to tension in your back, shoulders, and elsewhere even if you are performing strenuous labor all day. These are physical manifestations of the psychological strain you are under.

Many years ago I saw a presentation from a psychologist who had responded to numerous disasters. During his talk, he held up a container of canned asparagus. He told the audience that one of the body's responses to stress is fluid retention. And one effect of fluid retention is an enlargement of the discs in the spine, causing low-back pain. Asparagus is a natural diuretic, causing the body to urinate out extra fluid, diminishing the swelling, and relieving that pain. So this doctor always brought asparagus to an incident scene. It was a creative, if eccentric solution, to the stress-related back pain he had been experiencing. Stretching, yoga, and over the counter medications may be more mainstream answers to these problems. Find activities (or canned vegetables) for your list of coping mechanisms.

Physical
When in a disaster zone, your appetite may be diminished due to extreme heat and humidity, the tragedies you have witnessed, or guilt that your team has food and shelter and many locals do not. This is understandable. You are surrounded by people who are suffering. They may be injured, homeless, hungry from a shortage of food, or grieving lost loved ones. Many of them were desperately poor and hungry even before this catastrophe.

It is wise to acknowledge your feelings. You must then overcome any reluctance and make sure you are getting enough nutrition (at least 1500–2000 calories/day) and water/electrolyte solution (a minimum of 3–5 L/day) even if you don't feel hunger or thirst. Use your energy bars, dried fruit, trail mix, or nut butters as high calorie, nonrefrigerated options. Take a multivitamin to compensate for the lack of fresh fruits and vegetables in your diet. You are there to do a job and you will not be able to do so without the proper fuel.

Monitor your urine color and frequency—they are important indicators of your health. Your urine should be a shade of light yellow, similar to straw and you should need to relieve yourself every few hours. Dark urine is a sign of dehydration—drink more fluid! Urine that appears almost colorless may mean you are consuming too much water and not enough electrolytes, protein, and carbohydrates. No urine for an extended period of time, or other symptoms like a headache or cramps, probably means that you are badly dehydrated and need to stop what you are doing and hydrate before you collapse.

> **TIP**
>
> Your hiking/camping experiences should have given you an idea of your baseline fluid and nutrition needs while performing strenuous work. And, you should have brought the electrolyte drink mix, trail mix, energy bars, or other supplements that you found necessary for optimum performance.

Take special care with your personal hygiene. It can seem like too much effort to clean off the sweat, dust, sunscreen, insect repellent, mud, and other substances which have coated your body all day. Water for bathing will likely be room temperature or colder. It may have to be carried from afar and scooped from a bucket over your head, rather than flowing conveniently from a tap. Or, you may be relying on disposable moist towels because water is in such short supply. After a tough shift working in the heat, you may simply want to eat and collapse onto your sleeping mat. Resist the temptation!

Don't fall asleep without wiping or rinsing yourself first. Heat rashes, small cuts, and inflammations all become worse in grimy and sweaty conditions. Not to mention that you are working and living in extremely close quarters with your fellow volunteers. Even if you can't smell your own body odor, they probably can. Use deodorant every morning. Wash yourself every evening. Don't be the teammate people have to hold their breath near.

Ditto for clean uniforms. Putting on dirty clothes after washing yourself defeats the purpose behind bathing. You should have brought several changes of garments, as well as detergent, clothes-spins, and cord to hang items as they dry. Be proactive and wash your clothes before you have emptied your suitcase completely, so that you are always a shift or two ahead. This planning is especially important because in humid environments it may take 24 hours or more for your clean articles to dry and you'll be washing them in a bucket each night. A week or so into most deployments, we often find that locals offer to wash and fold our uniforms for a small fee. I think that's a great way to support the recovering economy and check another small but necessary task off the list.

BUILDING RELATIONSHIPS WITH YOUR LOCAL PARTNERS

As mentioned earlier, you will need local connections for many things including intelligence about areas of need, setting up an ongoing supply chain, laundry, food, etc. Be creative and open minded in your efforts to do so. Foster personal connections with them even if you are paying them for their services. Honor the thoughtfulness and generosity you will be experiencing from these traumatized residents.

In the Philippines we were given the use of several apartments whose occupants had left for the capitol a few days after the storm hit. We tried to treat those homes as we would our own, despite the primitive conditions without power and running water, and a rush to begin working. We stacked personal belongings and mementos in a closet so they wouldn't be lost or damaged as we spread our gear out. Soaked rugs were hung up to dry and we mopped away mud and sand.

No one wants to clean the bathrooms in a disaster. Because you're only going to be there a week or two, or you are tired and have more important duties, or it's difficult to find cleaning supplies. With many people are using them, restrooms quickly become disgusting. That situation is unhygienic for the current volunteers, disrespectful to the original owners, and highly demoralizing for your second team if they arrive at their new lodging to find toilets, sinks, and showers covered in any number of your substances.

After a day or two, set up a schedule and have a rotation of team members spend a few minutes a day cleaning. At the very least, clean on a weekly basis and when you are about to leave. If you are able to find a local who wants to do the job, similar to the laundry, pay them to do it. Be aware they will be in close proximity to your valuables, probably while you are out of the building working, so they will need to be vouched for and trustworthy.

The same hygiene issues occur in improvised community shelters because they have no training in shelter management. Communicate with the property owner or shelter organizer and suggest they set up a cleaning schedule. Often, with schools and businesses closed after a disaster, people will be sitting around anxious and stressed but bored. They may not be excited about cleaning bathrooms, sweeping up debris, and other menial tasks, but it will help pass the time and improve living conditions.

Your local contacts may offer to make you a meal, or to provide all your food. Like the laundry and cleaning, make sure you reimburse them for their time and supplies. It can be difficult for local cooks to accommodate dietary requests like gluten-free, paleo, vegetarian, or vegan. If there aren't local food sources, or you can't eat them, the food you brought may have to be your main source of energy for extended periods of time. As always, when traveling overseas, be cautious about eating fresh fruits and vegetables washed in possibly contaminated water.

You may be asked to, or end up, eating or drinking things you never expected. Try to handle these surprises gracefully. On a deployment, a group of young Chinese businessmen living in the apartment below us generously offered our team access to their Internet service. Many evenings, I would sit in their living room for an hour or more, using their connection to contact friends and family on my device. We didn't speak each other's languages and communicated with hand gestures. After a few nights, one of them handed me a glass filled with (what I thought was) an herbal liqueur that they had been drinking all week. I assumed there were roots and twigs marinating in the bottle they poured it out of. I was honored, but after a sip, and a closer look at the container, I realized the "roots" were actually dead seahorses marinating in whiskey. This was not something I wanted to continue drinking. Using sign language, I thanked the men for the gift but indicated that the drink was wasted on me and they should split the glass among themselves, which they did.

Some of the victims may want to share their disaster experiences with you. Others may not. Ask them the questions you need to fulfill your responsibilities ("How were you injured? How are you feeling? Where are you living?"). If you aren't trained in trauma counseling, let them take the lead talking about their situation. Don't press for details if you don't need them. Just be a caring human. Some might want to pray with you, which may make you uncomfortable if you are not religious. Put their needs first.

Lastly, I have found that making a gesture to the local people who have helped feed, shelter, and clean for us meant a great deal to them and to us. After a week in Tacloban, the residents of our building asked our team if we would set up a clinic for them one evening. They saw we were providing medical care to hundreds of their neighbors and wanted to be evaluated as well. We should have thought to offer that before they asked and it turned out to be a wonderful event. A few occupants needed routine medications but mostly it was a chance for our team to show our gratitude for their cooking, security, supplies, and friendship. If you can, organize a similar appreciation event for your local partners.

Children playing during rooftop clinic, Tacloban 2013. Photo Courtesy of Author.

PACKING UP, LESSONS LEARNED, LEAVING STUFF

After a week or two in the disaster zone, you will have accumulated a tremendous amount of valuable knowledge. You should be capturing these lessons in writing or some other format so you can share your experience with the team that is coming to replace you or to improve future responses with your organization.

During your deployment, ask yourself and your team what equipment and supplies you wish you had brought, and you should have left behind. Send this list to the incoming team. If you are the final group from your organization, bring these suggestions to your management, so they can be incorporated in future packing checklists and briefings.

Who were your key local partners? What were their priorities, fears, and strengths? Give the incoming team leaders an overview of the situation. During a disaster, we found that one of our most important local allies was very concerned about the perception that their organization was exploiting the catastrophe to bring in donations. Over the years, other charities in this country had been exposed wasting money and misusing resources. We had to reassure our new local friends that posting photographs and videos to ask for contributions for legitimate needs would not be seen as taking advantage of the situation. On the other hand, if they had made a unilateral decision not to publicize their efforts, we would have needed to respect that.

In addition to leadership level communication, find out who will be replacing each of the rest of your team. If you have the time and opportunity, message the person who will hold your position once they arrive. The times I have gotten a real-time report from someone on the ground, before I landed, it has given me a huge advantage in preparing for the deployment. If there is team already in the disaster zone, ask the organization if you can email your counterpart for a quick overview and suggestions.

When the new team arrives, they will be eager to begin work. We talked about the importance of a "tactical pause," so especially if you haven't had a chance to communicate with them before this, you should have a combined group briefing. Share the important information you have gained, including schedules of organizational meetings for your specialty such as the UN/WHO Health Cluster. Introduce them to the local partners. You may decide to donate personal or team equipment for them to use.

Rough mountain roads, Nepal 2015. Photo Courtesy of Author.

About leaving equipment or clothing in the disaster zone: make sure it has a use and a recipient. You will see that disposal of trash and debris is a huge issue for an area struggling to provide basic civic services. The victims probably do not need your old luggage or your worn out shoes, even if it makes the return trip easier. Take those items home.

Disaster Case Study:

Syria Conflict

In March 2011, as the movement known as the "Arab Spring" swept the Middle East, several teenagers were arrested for painting antiregime graffiti in the Syrian city of Deraa. Government forces fired upon subsequent street protests in the capitol of Damascus. Protests spread throughout the country and security services responded with increasing violence, causing dozens of deaths. Soon, the initial push to reform the current government changed to a movement to overthrow it. By July thousands of civilians had been killed and military defectors had begun setting up armed resistance.

Before the conflict, Syria was a nation of 18 million, with a heterogeneous population of mostly Sunni Muslims (75%), with Christian denominations, Kurds, and a variety of smaller ethnic groups making up the remainder. The country is 246.61 miles (396.88 km) wide and 282.89 miles (455.26 km) long. It borders Iraq, Israel, Jordan, Lebanon, Turkey, and the Mediterranean Sea. The government is ostensibly democratic but after Hafez al-Assad died in 2000, power passed to his son, Bashar al-Assad, in a presidential election with no opposition. From 1967 to 2011, Syria was under a continuous state of emergency rule giving the government extensive powers to ban gatherings and arrest opponents. Under both Hafez and Bashar al-Assad, the regime was accused of torture and other human rights violations.

From 2007 through 2010, socioeconomic and cultural tensions in Syria were intensified by a severe drought, an influx of 1.5 million refugees from Iraq and continuing economic "reforms" which disproportionately benefited regime supporters and the wealthy business class.

Syria has long been strategically important to the geopolitical conflicts between the United States, Russia, and countries in the Middle East. As the civil war widened, many of these players intervened to support their interests.

The fighting quickly splintered into factions including government forces backed by Russia, Hezbollah, Iran, and Iraq as well as armed groups from ISIL (the Islamic State in the Levant), the Kurdish independence movement, several religious minorities, and militias supported by the United States and Western Europe.

Syrian government combatants, in particular, have been accused of using indiscriminate bombing techniques (fuel air bombs) and chemical weapons (Sarin gas) against civilians and resistance fighters. ISIL has committed numerous documented atrocities, such as the kidnaping, torture and beheading of foreign aid workers and journalists, the mass rape of women and children, and suicide bomb attacks. Medical facilities and personnel as well as refugee aid organizations have been targeted by all sides.

The fighting is estimated to have caused upwards of 450,000 deaths by August 2016, as well as millions of serious injuries and immense psychological trauma to the population. As infrastructures such as hospitals, sanitation and drinking water systems were destroyed, a vast rise in infectious diseases such as hepatitis, diarrhea, leishmaniasis and formerly rare/controlled conditions such as polio occurred.

In addition to the deaths and injuries, nearly half the prewar population of Syria has been displaced from their homes as control of cities and neighborhoods shifted from faction to faction with increasing destruction over half a decade. More than 4 million people have sought refugee status outside the country. In turn, this exodus has stressed the governments and capacities of countries such as Lebanon, Jordan, Turkey, Greece, and Germany. These emigrants have faced physical danger as thousands drowned during attempts to cross the Mediterranean Sea as well as exploitation from human traffickers and corrupt employers in their new countries. As always, women, children, and the elderly are more vulnerable to every threat.

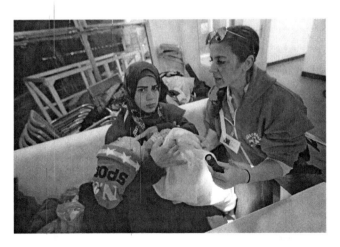

Syrian refugees being treated, Greece 2015. Photo Courtesy of Mike Morse Photography.

This massive man-made disaster has needed every type of humanitarian aid: medical care within the war zones and healthcare facilities for refugees in neighboring countries; mental health assistance; provision of food, water, and shelter; financial recovery; and even marine lifesaving missions for those attempting boat transits of the Mediterranean in poorly maintained and overcrowded vessels.

What role could you see for yourself in this catastrophe? Providing food and housing in a refugee settlement? Medical care, or psychological counseling, for those affected? Would you feel comfortable working in a war zone or prefer to work in a neighboring country? With the fears of terrorist activities, would your national security/police agencies understand if you went to Syria and then returned?

CHAPTER 9

Postdeployment

We cannot become what we want to be by remaining what we are.

Max De Pree

COMING HOME

You should continue to take any prophylactic medications, such as for malaria, on the flight back and for as long as prescribed. When leaving a region with poor water quality, many teams encourage their volunteers to take antiparasite tablets. As they cause cramps or diarrhea, it may be an uncomfortable trip home, so inform yourself about their side effects. On the other hand, you want to protect yourself, your family, and housemates from any foreign organisms you were exposed to.

Syrian Refugees arriving by boat, Greece 2015. Photo Courtesy of Mike Morse Photography.

How to Become an International Disaster Volunteer.

Similarly, wash all of your clothing, equipment, and luggage thoroughly upon your return. Sort through your gear and review your observations from the trip. Make notes about what should be added, removed, or repaired. Despite your tiredness, you should probably make these changes and then repack your deployment bag soon after coming home or you will forget that the air mattress has a small leak or a zipper was jammed. If you don't correct these issues now, you may suffer from them on your next disaster mission.

Psychologically, you may have anger and frustration about what could have been improved during the response: whether you did enough, or that your team could have worked more efficiently, or how society as a whole should have better assisted these victims. You might feel guilty about going home with people still suffering from homelessness, injuries, and grief there. You will be emotionally drained from the experience. These are all natural emotions. You can start to deal with them using the PsySTART tools. You may wish to seek professional counseling. Follow your own instincts when it comes to discussing the things you observed. For some responders, recounting their experiences is therapeutic. For others, that process retraumatizes them. Talk about your deployment when you are ready and if you are ready to do so. You shouldn't feel pressure to talk about it before you are emotionally prepared to.

I also encourage you to "continue" your response afterward by raising awareness and funds for the disaster. I found it to be meaningful to speak about my experiences to students or in a staff meeting at work. That made me feel my contribution to the disaster was ongoing instead of coming to an abrupt halt after 2−3 intense weeks abroad.

Physically, you will probably be exhausted. You may have slept poorly in a tent, or on a cot in a room full of snorers, often on a time zone opposite to your home. You might have been doing hard labor in hot and humid conditions, gradually become more tired each day. In conditions of living in group, volunteers often become ill with minor respiratory or gastrointestinal issues. You may have had several lengthy flights and layovers, traveling for 24 hours or more to get home.

Korean Disaster Response Team treating patients, Tacloban 2013. Photo Courtesy of Mike Morse Photography.

You will want to jump back into the old routine and make up for the work, classes, messages, and bills which have been waiting, but be gentle with your schedule and the readjustment into your day-to-day life. Try to give yourself a day or two to rest. Ration your "to-do" list to only one or two tasks a day on top of your work or school. You will also be busy reestablishing your relationships and telling friends and family about the deployment, if you choose to.

For me, everything at home feels slightly surreal after a disaster deployment. The hot showers and smooth roads are great but the "important" political news headlines seem foolish after the catastrophe I responded to. My friends' concerns about sports and celebrities seem shallow. I have a hard time focusing on mundane details. I now realize and accept that this is part of the readjustment process.

It may take months or years after your disaster response for your experiences to sink in. As that happens, you can ask yourself what's next.

- Was one deployment enough or would you like to do it again?
- If you want to do another disaster response, how long do you need to recover/prepare?
- Where are you in your professional, academic, or personal life and when/will you have the flexibility to make another deployment?
- If another international deployment isn't likely in the near future, could you serve in a domestic disaster relief organization? Or serve your community in some other way?

- What would you do differently or the same? Switching volunteer organizations, response focus (housing vs food vs medical), or region of the world?
- Did your deployment make you to change careers, your university major, or affect your relationships, faith or priorities?
- What life lessons, professional practices, or psychological/philosophical observations did you make/learn?
- If you are using these response experiences in your current career or educational track, how can you best communicate them?
- Could you see yourself as a full-time disaster responder? How would that affect your lifestyle and relationships?

To answer those questions, go back to your journal and start at the beginning. What motivated you to begin this process? Adventure? Service? Professional opportunities? How have you changed as a person since then? What feelings do you experience when you read your notes and look at your pictures from the deployment? Even if you don't show it to anyone, could you write an essay, or record a statement expressing the range of emotions from your first days of this saga until your return from this most recent deployment?

Whatever your answers to these questions, take pride in your deployment. You responded to a perilous situation to help victims in extreme need. Very few people can say that. Great job and thank you!

I recommend you stay in touch with members of your team, at least one or two of them, if not all. They are the only people on earth who really know what you experienced over there. If you are struggling with negative feelings, they may be too. If you want someone to laugh with about a ridiculous incident that occurred, they probably do too. Share pictures, set up a phone call every few months, check on them. And, if your experiences are like mine, you might find yourself on multiple deployments with some of the same faces. Your organization should initiate a postevent briefing several weeks or months after your return. It may be focused on the details of the response, but you should also be able to share your emotional state.

While it's your decision whether to keep your feelings and conclusions to yourself, people will want to hear them: your friends, your family, current and future employers. It's rare to meet someone who has responded to a disaster and your experiences will inspire them even if that attention embarrasses you. I found it added to my discomfort if I couldn't make a coherent statement of why I went and how it made me feel when someone asked me so. I think it's worth your time to create a list of lessons learned and observations you made. You may be sharing them with friends over a beer, in a job interview or in an entrance essay, but the opportunities will arise.

Be honest, especially as you analyze the deployment for your own needs. And you can decide whether someone else would benefit from your experiences: positive and negative. As I wrote this book, I was embarrassed to share my malaria pill nightmares, forgotten tent poles, need for snivel gear, and nearly expired passport stories, but hopefully you will now learn from these mistakes and others.

You also need to be patient. You may find that after a multiyear preparation period you are ready, trained, and willing, but have no international disaster to respond to. You catch yourself secretly hoping for one and then feeling guilty for doing so. Having the contacts and outlets to do volunteer and/or response work closer to home should also continue your development and let you find value in your preparations in the meantime.

As Jack Minton, the founder of the relief group Hope Force International, says: disaster response is a terrible privilege. We are seeing people when their existence has been uprooted, their family members are injured, missing, or dead, and their futures are in chaos. Yet, we have the honor of trying to get them through these terrible days and weeks and it is not impossible that our actions can truly change their lives. And indeed it cannot help but change our own.

Sunset, Tacloban 2013. Photo Courtesy of Mike Morse Photography.

In conclusion, thank you for pursuing your dream of becoming an international disaster volunteer. I wish you safe travels, meaningful duties, an enthusiastic team and sympathetic airline representatives who upgrade your seat and ignore your overweight luggage.

CPSIA information can be obtained
at www.ICGtesting.com
Printed in the USA
FFOW02n1540060717
37548FF

9 780128 044636